POWER AND THE THRONE

Charter 88, whose staff and students put together this
book, is a campaign for a democratic written constitution and a culture of citizenship for Britain. It started in
1988, on the 300th anniversary of the revolution of 1688.
It now has nearly 50,000 signatories and supporters.

DEDICATION

Power and the Throne is dedicated to

Charter 88's Local Groups
– The Constitution is National, Citizenship is Local –

to

Ian McEwan
who at the Charter's first convention on 14 July 1990
argued
'It is time to say Boo to the big goose'

and to

Arthur Newton
former ship's electrician
who as a member of the Charter 88 Council
representing the Manchester Local Group
proposed that we do something about the Monarchy
which resulted in the Conference of May 1993
and this book.

POWER AND THE THRONE

edited and introduced by
Anthony Barnett

V

VINTAGE

in association with Charter 88

Published by Vintage 1994

2 4 6 8 10 9 7 5 3 1

This collection Copyright © Charter 88 1994

The Copyright in each essay is owned by the
author

First published in Great Britain by Vintage 1994

Vintage
Random House, 20 Vauxhall Bridge Road, London SW1V 2SA

Random House Australia (Pty) Limited
20 Alfred Street, Milsons Point, Sydney
New South Wales 2061, Australia

Random House New Zealand Limited
18 Poland Road, Glenfield,
Auckland 10, New Zealand

Random House South Africa (Pty) Limited
PO Box 337, Bergvlei, South Africa

Random House UK Limited Reg. No. 954009

A CIP catalogue record for this book
is available from the British Library

ISBN 0099 39311 5

Typeset by Deltatype Ltd, Ellesmere Port, S. Wirral
Printed and bound in Great Britain by
Cox & Wyman, Reading, Berkshire

CONTENTS

HELENA KENNEDY QC

Preface

'WHEN THERE IS a select committee on the Queen the charm of royalty will be gone. Its mystery is its life. We must not let in daylight upon magic.'

This is the view of Walter Bagehot, the prime interpreter of the modern constitution, confident in 1872 that the British way of doing things was best. It was a time when account-ability and openness had little place in the vocabulary of political debate. Here in Britain, the drama of government and state took place behind a veil of uncertainty, with the blurred image of royalty the apotheosis of that tradition. The façade of a mystical monarchy was a happy device behind which the real machinery of government could function quietly and without too much scrutiny.

Bagehot's arguments, rehearsed in the nineteenth century, are still relied upon by constitutional traditionalists today. During a time of social upheaval, an apparently unchanging head can give a sense of stability: and to separate pomp from power provides a safeguard against political megalomania or dictatorship. The monarchy is also a visible symbol of unity in a nation, the pageantry capturing the people's imagination and cementing national pride. The royal family is supposed to be a presentation of ourselves behaving well!

Has the magic been dispelled? Has cruel light shattered the illusion? The fact that discussion is taking place at all is an indicator of a significant shift in public perception. Only a few years ago the most fleeting criticism of the monarchy brought forth accusations of treason and sedition against the Robespierres and Dantons of the day. The offender in my own childhood was Willie Hamilton, a Scottish Labour MP, who regularly mounted an assault on the 'parasitic royals' and was speedily disowned by his party. However, recent opinion polls have shown a remarkable seachange in attitudes to the Crown with not a Jacobin in sight.

Who is to blame? A new generation of feckless Royals who have confused Holyrood with Hollywood and brought the monarchy into disrepute? An *ancien régime* at the palace wilfully adhering to the old form of saying nothing and giving nothing away, particularly money, when the rest of the country is facing financial cutbacks and recession? A media which will feverishly publish stories of disintegrating marriages, sexual intrigue and lavish spending, all in pursuit of increased circulation figures?

Rounding up the culprits is a pleasant distraction from a more profound cause of public malaise. The political stagnation of the last fifteen years has highlighted many of the failings of our constitution. People may not be holding forth on the role of Black Rod or the wielding of the royal prerogative but they are expressing real dissatisfaction with the Cabinet's seemingly endless quest for more power, more secrecy and less accountability, manifest so clearly in the Matrix-Churchill affair. There is disenchantment with almost every pillar of British life: Parliament, the House of Lords, the City, Lloyds, the Law, the police, the Church. There is growing distrust of politicians generally and serious doubt about the workings of our institutions. Evidence of decay seems to be all encompassing. The Crown, a naturally secretive institution, is almost guilty by association. Its position at the political and social apex makes it a ready symbol of an unfair and ineffective system.

Our constitution is unwritten, our rights exist within the silence of the law, appointments are made within a fog of unknowing and the British disease of secrecy seeps into every institutional corner. The political convenience of 'don't tell them, unless we really have to' has been honed into grandiose principles of governance, whose defenders invoke history, tradition and past success as reasons for leaving well alone. The checks and balances established in the past no longer provide equilibrium in the pre-millennium British state. An Upper House which is largely based on heredity is absurd and a mockery of the democratic principles which we are advocating for the rest of the world. The royal prerogative powers which are far more extensive than people realise can be used by the Executive without the possibility of challenge. The constitutional implications of European integration are only now beginning to filter through the blather of political rhetoric and the need for a clear written constitution is becoming a necessity.

For a long time it was fashionable to regard the Palace as a charming irrelevance: good for tourism and diplomacy and cheap at twice the price. But an institution which is accorded prominence and mythical status, which surrounds itself with the unworthy notion of aristocracy, keeps the hierarchical nature of our society firmly in place. It is understandable that many see it as the fountainhead of snobbery and class division, creating a corrosive culture with its defenders often sycophantically allied to its continuance because patronage is one of the pegs which secures its hold. Indeed, even the value for money argument is no longer very convincing to many citizens, who would have been so easily wooed had unprompted royal benevolence saved London Zoo or a royal endowment retained the Elizabeth Garrett Anderson as a special hospital for women. Instead, in the wake of public discontent, a rather belated arrangement for tax payment came to light and royal advisers cobbled together a plan to finance the rebuilding of Windsor that would be gentler on the public purse.

Any debate about the role of monarchy in the late twentieth century inevitably raises important questions about the way our system works. When the Queen gave her memorable Guildhall speech in 1992, it was naturally her striking Dryden-style allusion to the royal 'annus horribilis' that captured public attention. Yet the more significant aspect of her address was her acknowledgement that 'criticism is good for people and institutions that are part of public life'.

Charter 88 has never advocated the abolition of the monarchy. Amongst its members are both republicans and strong loyalists but the common bond of the signatories is a concern about the state of the country, a concern which reaches beyond party allegiance. There is a shared feeling that our institutions are no longer serving us well and that we need to create some architectural changes in the political edifice if we are to generate new ideas.

The debate which Charter 88 hosted with the *Times* newspaper was a great event. Many views were expressed and not all are included here. Not only did it break the taboo about even discussing the Queen's role, it made clear that many of our institutions, national practices and cultural habits are affected by and intertwined with the monarchy. It was also an event which proved that discussions about the constitution need not be bone-achingly dull and lawyer-ridden. It was exciting and it was fun. It was also only the start, as is this book. There are many more voices to be added to the arguments. Constitutional change is an idea whose time has come. It is not about abandoning the past but building upon British tradition and history to create a modern system which is efficient, engaging and just.

ANTHONY BARNETT

THE EMPIRE STATE

'IT'S UP TO the people to stand up and shout. Not to turn it into cynicism, which is what is happening. Politics is still crucially important. Our choices are vital, and we've got to make them and not just say, oh, they're all the same.'

> Dennis Potter in his last interview.
> April 1994.

AS BRITAIN ENTERED the nineties it seemed to many that the Royal Family had come to symbolise 'the British disease'. Scandal, divorce, tax avoidance, heavy leaking to the tabloids, claims to undemocratic privilege and loss of prestige – a pervading sense of tawdriness, disenchantment and impoverishment exuded from the Royal Household. It led commentators to suggest that it had become a reflection of the British disease of economic disappointment, lack of direction and a felt loss of the future.

There may be a British disease. But there is also British wealth, energy, inventiveness, humour, and improvement. Were this not so arguments about the monarchy would be nothing more than disputes between receivers and curators over the disposition of a bankrupt museum-nation. Many of us refuse such a fate, hence the conference this book of essays is drawn from. But a great many of our political class, especially among its two main political parties and the mandarins of Whitehall, are fixated on preservation. Preservation, that is, of the system of sovereignty that gives them absolute legal power, embossed by the Royal Coat of Arms and protected by the constitution.

Few people in Britain express the slightest interest in the

constitution – at the moment. Most, if asked about it, say they are not qualified to have a view. Those who feel they are better informed might dryly, if mistakenly, comment that the UK does not have a constitution at all. Yet everyone, even if despite themselves, talks about the monarchy. They may laugh at it, they may defend it, they may *insist* it is unimportant or argue that it is 'the only thing that keeps our country *Great*'; they might despair at the triviality of it all or fear the reactions of others if the subject is raised, they may recall the Blitz or admire the Queen for the job she does: but whether it is anger or loyalty, love it or hate it, everyone feels something about the Royal Family and can say so. No one says, as they do about the constitution, 'I'm simply not qualified to have a view'.

The same goes for journalists and commentators. The people who in 1988 assured the fledgling Charter 88 that the constitution was irrelevant and of no interest to their readers and viewers, filled the media with lengthy reports packed with mind-boggling detail on the constitutional implications of the royal separation of Charles and Diana. They did so confident that people would read or watch them and that their colleagues would acknowledge the relevance of their words.

This contrast touches the heart of something. What are we to make of a country where on the one hand a single maladjusted family matters to everybody, yet on the other almost no one can articulate an opinion about how as a country we govern ourselves? The purpose behind this book is to break the spell: to terminate the displacement that leads us to indifference towards what does matter and obsession with what does not. We need to end the diversion of attention invested in the monarchy and allow the energy to flow back to issues worthy of our attention. Not least because current chat about the Queen enforces our participation in a poor bargain. It is our way of reproducing the unwritten constitution, of consenting to a closed and secretive society. When we say 'we are bored by the constitution', or 'it is not for us', we agree to government continuing in the old way.

It is hard to break the spell. I am trying to draw attention to something which makes itself invisible – 'boring' – as you call attention to it. For example, a common assumption accompanies our unwritten arrangements and often blinds us as to their breadth and relevance. This is that the moment you start to talk about the constitution it is taken to be a 'specialist' matter about such things as whether the Queen would be politicised if there was a hung parliament. Perhaps because the British Constitution is unwritten its influence is hard to grasp. So its role is presumed to be concerned with such details of constitutional law. The power *of* a constitution, however, is much greater and has an impact on everyone. The power of a constitution is different in kind from the powers exercised within it.

This is understood, if instinctively, by the political elite *for whom*, it can be said, the constitution is unwritten. They help to preserve the status quo by interpreting questions about the constitution as being about their decisions, not human rights. One senior member of the Establishment told the modern historian Peter Hennessy that the British Constitution is 'something we make up as we go along'.[1] Ask yourself who this 'we' is, and you begin to understand the power of a constitution: it is less about the rules than about who makes and who can break them.

Winner Takes All

The time to get angry about the British Constitution is overdue. It was already time during the last Labour Government when on 20 July 1976 Michael Foot, in his position as Leader of the House, put through five guillotine motions in one day.[2] Foot had a reputation as a great liberal parliamentarian. The guillotines rammed policy through and curtailed scrutiny, an attitude towards the Commons which prepared the way for Mrs Thatcher.

It was time to get angry then and again ten years later when Margaret Thatcher forced through the Community Charge, or Poll Tax, that levied local government charges on a per capita basis. This meant that a poor family with two young people and an infirm grandparent could pay five times as much in local tax as a wealthy property owner with a house ten times larger.

Discontent with the Poll Tax helped to make Mrs Thatcher sufficiently unpopular for her to be removed from office by her own party. Afterwards as the General Election results came through in 1992, Mrs Thatcher commented ruefully (or perhaps defiantly) that they proved that her Poll Tax worked after all. Because, she reckoned, it had removed a million people from the electoral register. This was an exaggeration. It probably removed about 350,000 – more than enough, however, to ensure the Conservatives a working majority.[3]

Apart from the *Sunday Telegraph*, no paper picked up her remark or publicised it, and Labour failed to respond promptly by insisting upon a voting system that really ensured all citizens could vote. And the former Prime Minister's remarks confirmed a deeper wrongdoing. A principal argument *against* the Poll Tax was that it was fundamentally undemocratic. By identifying residents through the use of the electoral register it was a tax on suffrage – which in America would have made it unconstitutional. In Britain the fact that it would disenfranchise poorer people was known and discussed by the Prime Minister and her advisers at the time it was introduced, and was considered a justification *for* the Poll Tax. The gerrymandering of local elections in, say, Westminster is as nothing to the gerrymandering of the entire electoral system consciously undertaken and then passively permitted and retrospectively condoned by those who run and report on British affairs.

These are just two examples from Foot and Thatcher of the *use* of power allowed by the British Constitution that might have been recognised and prevented as an *abuse* of power if we had a written constitution. The exceptionally unrestrained power exercised by the British Government stems from 'The absolute sovereignty of Parliament'. At its heart is the assertion that there can be only one centre of power, one 'Leviathan' to keep us in order. It is a glamorous, royal notion that executive power cannot be shared and that after an election 'winner takes all'. Even if it worked it would be abhorrent. But it doesn't. It is increasingly incompatible with the realities of contemporary society.

Britain's governing elite damages the centres of our cities, our countryside, our local government, our rights, our industries, our jobs, our standing in Europe, our traditions of tolerance, and it does so despite overwhelming popular support for many if not all these things. You name it, they'll abolish it. Unless, that is, you name 'the sovereignty of parliament'. Then they will go weak at the knees, sing songs of praise to the 'mother of democracy', and hide behind the skirts of the Queen.

The lure of absolute sovereignty exercises a compelling spell over the British political classes and through them over the British public. This is the central reason why the monarchy is as all-important as it is all-pervading: I mean by this *not* the individuals who bear or await the Crown, but first the policy failures and second the culture which radiates from the presence of the throne and penetrates everywhere through the desire for peerages, the honours system, snobbery, social connections and deference, and also their associated opposites of equally mindless defiance and exasperation.

What is a Constitution?

We are held in the framework of a constitution as powerful as it is old. The fact that it is 'unwritten' does not mean that we do not have one. All countries have a constitution. Furthermore, the constitutions of all countries everywhere are *both* written and unwritten.

When it is said that in Britain we have an unwritten constitution, it means there is no codified set of 'basic laws' with a special status, no laws that are harder to change than ordinary law. We have no fundamental rule book that sets out the purpose, aims, objectives and means of government, including how the mass of everyday laws are made or unmade. There is no description of the distribution of power or of the nature of people's rights. There are written laws in Britain, codes of practice and historic institutions which can be seen as constitutional. Unlike most other countries in the world, however, they are not drawn together by a single document.

Britain is an exception in this. But the constitutions of all countries are also in important ways partly unwritten. This is because all constitutions are lived. Suppose two countries have written constitutions that are *identical* word for word: one has a historic tradition of respect for rights and an independent and relatively honest police force, the other is dominated by a militant religion, has few lawyers and combines police and army under a single political command. Clearly, the way the two countries will be governed would be very different. As Christopher Hitchens points out, the constitution of Liberia is modelled on that of the United States. What is *made* of a constitution by those who live with it is *more* important than the paper it is written upon. If there is no independent judiciary, no rooted local government, no tradition of free speech, no financially independent publishers, then the public will not be able to claim its rights or check abuses of power. In all countries it is the attitudes, behaviour, culture and traditions – the necessarily and thankfully unwritten realities – that breathe life into written constitutions, or, like the empty caricatures of Soviet-style constitutions, turn them into dead letters.

The relationship between what is in writing and what is made of what is written depends on many factors, above all the institutions that exercise power and the spirit of the people. Take the question of 'openness'. Whether a society is open or is closed to change is vital to its future. The UK's unwritten constitution is singled out for praise by its defenders because, they say, it is flexible, unlike a written constitution which they allege would be rigid. In fact most people experience the British system as closed and secretive, rooted in a citadel of absolute sovereignty while a new constitution with a democratic, public document would be open to change.

Defined in this way as a set of governing principles both written and lived, a constitution has three main aspects.

The first concerns the relationship between the individual and the State and the individual and lesser authorities. This relationship establishes what rights, freedoms and entitlements an individual has or does not have, from the right to speak or worship, for example, to the right to associate, to be housed or educated, and whether these are indeed rights of citizenship or not. Some rights are dedicated to minorities, to protect them from the majority, although the majority also has a self-interest in protecting minorities. But rights are also for everyone. They enhance our sense of pride and dignity in ourselves and our society. As Tom Paine wrote two hundred years ago in *The Rights of Man*, 'A Declaration of Rights is, by reciprocity, a Declaration of Duties also. Whatever is my right as a man, is also the right of another; and it becomes my duty to guarantee, as well as to possess.'[4]

The second aspect of all constitutions concerns the distribution of power between different centres of authority. If, for example, there are two parliamentary chambers their power relative to one another; if there are parliaments outside the national one, whether they have federal rights of their own, or are absolutely subordinate; who fixes elections and by what principles; what power voters have if, as in some constitutions, they can be consulted through referenda; what powers and obligations a constitutional court has to resolve disputes between different centres of authority or between individuals seeking to enforce their rights against authority.

While the first broad aspect of a constitution concerns individual rights, this second area concerns powers. Lord Scarman has written that constitutions ensure four basic safeguards for society.[5] The first is that of individual rights. The other three are: the clear specification of legislative and executive power; the protection of regional and local power; and an independent judiciary empowered to protect the constitution. All three come under this second heading of powers.

In addition to *rights* and to *powers* there is a third aspect to every constitution, *aspirations*. 'Life, liberty and the pursuit of happiness', the principles first inscribed in the American Declaration of Independence are a notable example. This aspect of a country's constitution is more difficult to define because it itself is concerned with definition, with the purpose, aims and values – whether or not these are formally declared in the preamble to the constitution itself.

In Britain's heyday its unwritten constitution embraced a strong code. It presumed that its administration would be carried out with the probity and integrity one would expect of a Christian country. Empire implied duty, and its codes really meant something, they literally *governed* the public behaviour of many. And if a gentleman's word was his bond and one didn't need two lawyers to put it in writing for both sides, then this was a wonderful asset also for the success of the City as a marketplace for efficient business.

The values to which a country aspires and which in turn govern its public servants include a characterization of the kind of people it wants its citizens to be, for example, free, united or obedient to God or to Allah. Such national ideals may be inscribed in the preamble to a written constitution, or they may be embedded in a national religion or represented by a national institution such as a monarchy. A country's aspirations are also bound up with the way its national identity seeks to define who is or is not loyal and how the country is different from its neighbours, for a country's constitution and its nationalism go hand in hand.

This three-fold definition describes the *overall* nature of a constitution as a framework for the way a country works. The content of a law is a legal question; the nature of public access to the law is constitutional. The policy that a government legislates is political; whether that policy can be challenged in the courts is constitutional. The preparation of policy decisions by the civil service is administrative; how civil servants are answerable for their actions is constitutional. The way criminal laws are implemented is a question of policing; whether policing is fair for everyone is constitutional.

The purpose of writing down a constitution should be to improve, equalise and democratise the implementation of rules: to enhance peoples' rights and their respect for the rights of others, and to aid the effective and efficient sharing of power and resolution of conflicts. The paper on which it is written should help to bring the principles of justice to life. Let me emphasise the word 'should'. Of course the purpose of a dictator in writing down a country's constitution is further to humiliate and mislead the population, whose constitutional reality is dictatorship, even if fine-sounding constitutions can be turned against such authors. So the assessment of a constitution best begins by looking at the inter-relationships of the three main parts. To what extent are the aspirations honestly found in the institutions and laws that distribute power and ensure people their rights?

Aspirations and the Throne

Taking this broad definition of a constitution the monarchy's role becomes clearer. It would be a 'mere decoration' only if the country already had a set of written constitutional principles that commanded general allegiance. Instead, in Britain an increasingly isolated monarchy occupies almost all of the third aspect of our constitution. It was, and wishes to remain, the representative of our country's unity and aspirations. There are many references to this role in the essays that follow. They make it clear that officially Britain's hopes for the future are supposed to be embedded in the monarchy. I will prove the point with one example: a recent, passionate defence by William Waldegrave, who says that the mighty symbolism of the monarchy gives us a vision of what we should be.

Educated at Eton, a Fellow of the elite Oxford college of All Souls, currently a senior Cabinet Minister and a man of integrity who would have been at home in earlier Tory administrations, Waldegrave has been responsible for some original if strained constitutional innovations. He is the first Minister for 'Open Government', his brief being to make sufficient concessions to block a Freedom of Information Act. He is also in charge of the 'Citizen's Charters'. To defend them he has argued that people prefer the trains to be punctual rather than vote, as if the two activities are opposed to each other. Useful so far as they go, it would have been more truthful if he had renamed the Citizens' Charters 'Subject's Remedies'. Underlying his approach is a more serious project, to turn the electorate into customers rather than citizens, so

9

that they relate to the state as consumers and not as its proprietors.

Turning to the monarchy in the columns of the *Sunday Telegraph*, Waldegrave wrote that it was essential to prevent the throne from being undermined.[6] For it 'embodies a concept of service to something above and beyond ourselves ... It is not to the fellow human being that we bow our heads, or in whose name our laws are made; it is to the mighty symbols we have asked them to embody for us that we pay allegiance'. 'Future subjects', should not criticise Prince Charles's personal problems, for 'he will be our King'. Nor is this just a matter of personal concern. We will need the monarchy 'more not less in the future ... if we are to keep our sanity and sense of community ... By carrying the symbols of our highest traditions, its representatives help us to have a vision of what we should be'.

Nothing he has written on the Citizens' Charters echoes the force and conviction of these sentiments. Waldegrave's defense of open government is hedged with half-closed prose. His Charters could be issued on prescription, as a guaranteed non-addictive substitute for sleeping pills. *They* do not contain a vision of what we should be. But if you believe Waldegrave on the monarchy, it will be hard to sleep this side of the coronation of Charles III – as he reminds us without hesitation or embarrassment that we are subjects.

The tension in William Waldegrave's argument is palpable. On the one hand claiming that the Royal Family gives us a vision of what we should be and on the other informing us that as the world speeds forward, we must cling to monarchy for the sake of our sanity. If the latter is what it is about, it has ceased to embody Britain's global aspirations and has become instead a security blanket (embroidered with the word 'community').

The monarchy we know today was reformed and made popular in the late nineteenth century with great ceremonies, such as the State Opening of Parliament.[7] This 'invention of tradition' was in no way experienced as a nostalgic exercise in preserving sanity. On the contrary, for the Victorians it was a

10

dramatic and novel means of expressing British purpose and prowess, of claiming a world role. I will return to this formative period when the institutions were developed which together can be called the 'Empire State'. The monarchy then successfully embodied the aspirations of its country and fulfilled the third aspect of Britain's imperial constitution, symbolising it as a whole. Yet it was not alone in so doing. It was an organic expression for a new, popular imperial regime: the keystone to an arch of institutions, financial, commercial and military, that spanned the world.

Now the monarchy no longer symbolises a system of power that offers, as it then arguably did, an honest, effective and enriching form of government, that protected British liberties and called on British loyalties in war and peace. It has ceased to be a coherent representative of contemporary realities. A large gap has opened up between its values and our society's realities, a chasm which is also a constitutional crisis. For the monarchy has now become a symbol for the resistance to reform by the politicians who occupy the throne of winner-takes-all-politics and utilise its powers and prerogatives for themselves. We cannot confront them, we cannot democratise the British system, until we first separate out the role of the Crown.

I began with a complaint about the way everyone can talk about the Royal Family. It might have seemed a graceless way to introduce a collection of essays on the monarchy. In fact this collection marks a larger breakthrough which can be greeted with relief. It marks the fact that, perhaps for the first time since 1914, we can argue in a healthy way about the constitutional role of the monarchy, connecting this to the substantive problems of power and democratic government in Britain.

To further this debate I want to look first at the monarchy itself, then move on to consider the system of power that it heads, which I've termed the 'Empire State' and conclude by describing the two main alternatives now lining up to challenge the Empire State in its English homeland.

Ironically, the alternatives can be represented by Charter 88 and by Rupert Murdoch's media empire, whose paper *The Times* sponsored the Charter 88 conference on 'The Monarchy, the Constitution and the People', held on 22 May 1993 which inspired this book. The collaboration of Charter 88 and *The Times* may seem curious and unlikely. On the one hand, the newest non-government organisation in town, Charter 88 is an anti-establishment campaign dedicated to becoming a full-scale citizens' movement that doubles and redoubles its nearly 50,000 strong support. Its aim: a democratic, written constitution created by popular demand and leading to a culture of citizenship rather than subjecthood. On the other hand, the oldest daily paper, the news-sheet of the Establishment itself that weighs what it regards as the larger interests of the nation. Yet both share a desire to see the institutions scrutinised and reformed in the context of constructive debate. Granting all disagreements, there is a common support for pluralism and freedom of speech as against fundamentalism and political correctness. This allowed a joint debate to open on the monarchy.

A Vision for the People

It is important to recognise that the monarchy itself has certainly worked hard at being a vision for the people. Thanks to television especially it managed since 1945 to keep up its constitutional function as the embodiment of British aspirations in a changing world.

In 1953 the young Queen's coronation was celebrated as the dawn of no less than 'The New Elizabethan Age'. It came after Labour had been forced from office in 1951, demoralised and deeply split. The Conservatives under Churchill accelerated the abolition of post-war rationing then celebrated a renewal of the old order, now a welfare Empire State but safely in Conservative hands. The young sovereign graced it with hope and insisted that the Coronation be filmed and televised. It was a watershed for the new medium. TV sets acquired for the purpose, or watched at the neighbours, entered peoples' homes across the country, never to leave. It was a 'shared experience' of a new kind for Britain. Television anointed the nation with its special destiny. The Empire State was beautiful, electronic and in its twenties.

In 1969 a BBC TV documentary *Royal Family* presented Britain with a different kind of intimacy, watched, it is claimed, by sixty-eight per cent of the population. Colour television brought the images of royalty even more closely into our homes, images that were no longer of ceremonies of state but of the people themselves in *their* home 'like us'. The film was traditional Britain's response to the sixties. A 'normal' family life deeply worthy of emulation was presented to the nation in contrast to the long hair and libertine irresponsibility of swinging London, whose alternative forms of colour, music and incense were officially rebuked. Millions were deeply grateful.

A third moment of redefining representation came with the royal wedding of the heir to the throne to Diana in 1981. Even younger than the Queen in 1953, Lady Di with her long legs and obvious enjoyment of non-royal activities such as shopping, was a renewal of a new kind. Ill-educated and modern in her style, her rise seemed to symbolise the end of restrictive practices and the aspirations of the early Thatcher era: that competition and personal ambition would unleash energy and wealth and reverse Britain's decline.

Impossible Embodiment

The belief that a monarch can personalise the condition of the nation is as old as monarchy itself. Sophocles's great tragedies of Oedipus are an example and draw on stories that pre-date 500BC. When the plague struck Thebes, the oracle told King Oedipus and his people that to be saved they had to deal with the source of their corruption, namely the murderer who had killed their previous king and who still lived amongst them unpunished. Hearing this, Oedipus swears to unmask and punish the regicide, only to embark upon an appalling confrontation with the truth. A holy prophet tells Oedipus: 'the curse that corrupts the Kingdom is You'. Soon Oedipus discovers that he himself was the killer. Then, that his victim was biologically his own father. And thus that his wife, Queen to them both, is his mother. Bursting with agony he blinds himself. Too shamed ever again to look upon his beloved city or his children, he dashes out his eyes.

Who would want to say to Queen Elizabeth II what the holy man, the blind prophet Tiresias, told Oedipus that: 'The curse that corrupts the Kingdom is You'? The answer is, not even today's republicans like Stephen Haseler who politely ask her to lay down the Orb and Sceptre so that her leaving the throne will become her. The transformative power of the modern media gives us a sense of intimacy which means we would all sense the injustice of such an accusation. We might well expect her to echo Oedipus's own plea of mitigation: 'All these were things I had to suffer. They were thrust upon me against my will, I am not guilty. It was not my choice that my Uncle was obliged to abdicate, and so place me in line to the throne. It was not my choice that I should be crowned young, and full of promise. It was not I who cheered and celebrated a new monarchy to the echo, past the half-way mark of the twentieth century. It was not I who decided to rid this country of its great Empire that I was trained and asked to rule. It was not I who voted for the governments who have done so much harm. All this you did to me. All this I received as a gift. A prize to break the heart.'

Indeed, it can be proved that the problem with the monarchy does not lie with the life-style of the Royal Family. The public adoration of royal magic began during the second half of the long reign of George III. Britain fought and defeated the French in the revolutionary wars but felt besieged. It needed a figurehead. Though the King was regarded as insane and the behaviour of his children appalling, their all too human failings became evidence of majestic humanity: 'George III's . . . severe bouts of illness, his encroaching age and his bevy of dissolute sons seem not so much to have detracted from the reputation of the monarchy, as to have increased public protectiveness towards the King himself. By being manifestly vulnerable, he became more not less appealing.'[8]

If the nation wants to rally to its symbolic head of state, a royal family can do no wrong. For whatever wrong it does will be interpreted as evidence of its sublime royalty. Similarly, it does not matter how 'good' the monarch is when people cease to believe – when they begin to realise that there is something rotten in the state, and it isn't Denmark. Then, if the monarch goes on television he or she is accused of exposing themselves to public contempt and lessening the majesty of the office. If they do not, they are accused of undermining their appeal through remoteness and presumption. There is no way to win if you are the symbol of a losing constitution.

Equally, attacking the individuals for being bad at being symbolic is futile and beside the point, it draws attention away from the real problem: the system of power and authority that can no more command credibility. In his study of the monarchy Anthony Holden quotes the former editor of *Spectator*, Alexander Chancellor, who asks 'is there any aspect of the Windsor family, with its broken marriages and its burning palaces that can still be held up to Britain as an example of how things ought to be?'[9] This is one of the milder of personal criticisms. For not taking up this theme at The Monarchy Conference, Charter 88 was accused by Michael White of the *Guardian* of 'tiptoeing' round the issue. But Charter 88 is right not to set itself up as a pulpit to 'criticise' the monarchy. Such talk is no criticism of the institution at all. On the contrary, whingeing about their life-style, tittering about their personal phone-calls, or snorting at their clumsy public relations, are all signs of dependency, not independence of mind. Such talk is evidence of self-subordination.

You Trust Us

As no one can be good at symbolising a rotten constitution there is no point in accusing the Royals of failure, or of being somehow responsible for what is going wrong. Equally, there is little point in the monarchy attempting to restore its standing within the confines of the existing system.

Such an attempt is being made. On Sunday 24 January 1993, the *Mail on Sunday* led with a banner story: MY CONCERN, THE QUEEN, by Adrian Lithcoe its political correspondent. It announced:

> First moves to improve the standing of the monarchy have been ordered by the Queen. She has asked senior courtiers and advisors to conduct far-reaching soundings about the relationship between the palace and the people . . . The Queen's Lord Chamberlain, Lord Airlie, her assistant private secretary, Sir Kenneth Scott and her Press Secretary, Charles Anson, have started talking with respected figures in public life. They will consider not only the monarchy and the people, but also the City, the Church of England, the Houses of Parliament, the legal establishment, the military hierarchy, the press and the police . . . the advisers will prepare a report amounting to a blueprint of how to reestablish the bond between Britain's institutions and its people.

This was quite a scoop. The key concept in the royal investigation was 'Trust'. Lithcoe quotes a 'royal insider' who explains the approach:

> People continue to claim (the royal adviser told him) that Britain is riddled with class. It is not, but the cement of our society is trust. When the police are trusted as little as politicians, and the morale of the Church of England is so low and the monarchy itself might be in some jeopardy, it is time to ask ourselves, 'What are we doing wrong?'

You might say that it is time for the British people to ask 'What wrong is being done to us?'. The *Mail on Sunday* concluded by reporting that 'Buckingham Palace said last night. . . that specific talks were not taking place on the future of the constitution itself'.

There are two especially interesting aspects to this story. The first concerns the nature of 'trust' as perceived by the Palace. It is a one-way street, or rather, because the image is vertical, trust is upwards. The downward attitude, with its secrecy and confidential soundings, is *distrust*. The blueprint for reestablishing 'the bond between Britain's institutions and its people' will not be shared with the people. The aim is to reestablish the people's faith in the monarchy, not, it goes without saying, the monarchy's faith in the people.

Second, the reassurance given by the Palace to the *Mail on Sunday* that the future of the constitution was not under review is a wonderful giveaway. For what else *is* the relationship between the Monarchy, the people, the City, the Church, parliament, the law, the military, the media and the police, *but* the constitution? Here we can witness the enforcement of the taboo at first hand. While the air may be full of royal talk, discussion of the constitution – the realities of power – must be avoided. Because once the constitution is openly admitted to be in play, why then there would have to be a dialogue. The Palace can get away with keeping to itself its blueprints on reestablishing 'trust'. But if it admitted that it had ordered a blueprint on the future of the constitution it would be our constitution too, and the public would feel they had a right to know what it contained.

It has to be said, however, that the Queen's attitude is considerably healthier than that of Michael Portillo. Currently a Treasury minister, Portillo has been selected by Mrs Thatcher as her favoured successor for No 10. When the Queen, in her Guildhall speech of November 1992, described that year as an 'annus horribilis', she argued that 'No institution – City, Monarchy, whatever – should expect to be free from the scrutiny of those who give it their loyalty and support, not to mention those who don't.' A year later, in a keynote speech, Portillo denounced all such criticism as 'self-doubt and cynicism'.[10] These, he proclaimed, were the new 'enemy within', one more insidious than the Cold War itself because 'self-doubt gnaws away at the sinews of our institutions and weakens the nation'. The Royal Family provides Portillo with the clearest example of an institution under threat from criticism. 'But the point of the monarchy', he argues, 'is that it is the source of the authority and legitimacy of government'. So much for elections, which presumably are today merely decorative. 'Above all', Portillo concludes, the monarchy 'is an institution vital to our national well-being' because it is 'the personification of the nation'. The danger could hardly be greater and therefore we must 'throw out' such defeatism even if it means that 'we must temper our traditional tolerance'.

After 15 years of unprecedented exercise of power, a leading Thatcherite declares that the country is in peril due to cynical critics supported by unnamed pressure groups. Only a desperate fight back can save Britain from their insidious power. Who are they? Jon Snow pressed Portillo in a Channel 4 interview; reasonably enough, given that Portillo claimed to have uncovered 'one of the greatest threats that has ever confronted the British nation'. Could the Minister do us the service of naming two or even one such source of danger? He declined.

Which was a pity because his speech is helpful in clarifying the arguments over how we can 'reassert the value and the quality of the British way of life'. The Portillo approach is to insist on the value of the *institutions* as 'vital to our national well-being', and to argue that we must sacrifice our traditions, such as tolerance, to preserve them. The alternative approach argues that if we wish to conserve positive British *traditions*, of tolerance, probity, freedom, fairness and successful enterprise, then we have to reform our institutions.

The Palace seems much less rigidly inclined than Portillo to insist on its own untouched preservation. This is not simply thanks to its divine sensitivity to the populace. The monarchy has seen society revolutionised since 1945 and the institutions and social forces that surround it fall away. The buttresses that supported the cathedral of royalty have crumbled. Great historical developments, not changes in elite opinion, have left it isolated and exposed. It surely knows this at least. The Palace may not trust the people, but after more than a decade with Mrs Thatcher, the Royal Family would have good reason to trust even less the prospect of finding itself in the last trench with Michael Portillo, who transparently desires to use the Crown to legitimate his own personal ambitions.

The Buttresses: The Church and Male Clubs

In order to grasp how the twentieth century revolution in British society has affected the monarchy we can conduct our own brief and partial survey of the crumbling buttresses starting with the Church that it heads. I have emphasised that all constitutions, written or unwritten, are lived. They embody a social ethic, a set of values about how laws are carried out in life. In the United Kingdom the carrier of these values, loyal to God, Crown and Empire, was the self-disciplined, middle class of 'Christian gentlemen' and their wives, who sent their children to Sunday school and the Boy Scouts and Girl Guides. From schoolmaster and shopkeeper to skilled craftsman, the ideal of the Christian gentleman, from Catholic to Quaker, embodied the traditions that upheld the British Constitution.

The fact that there can be any question about whether the monarch should continue to head the Church of England is evidence of the collapse of this traditional constitutional order. The Church has been obliged to respond. Easy to mock, it has embraced modernisation, far and away the most significant index of which is the decision to allow the ordination of women. The scenes of jubilation that greeted the vote of the Synod, the Church's governing assembly, when it approved of women priests, suggest deep and motivated enthusiasm for the reform. It was carried by more than a two-thirds majority of all three sections of the Synod: its lay members, the clergy and the bishops. (We can note in parentheses how familiar the British are with written constitutions in every activity except the State.)

Equality for women is the first measure of modern democracy. I mean by this something more than nominal equality of voting rights, even if this must come first. I mean the actual presence of women in *positions* of power and influence. It is a primary measure because, while difficult enough, it is easier to achieve than social and economic justice, or the integration of ethnic minorities. One of the unifying features of the Empire State that linked its top members together into a single universe was the exclusion of women. A similar, leather armchair atmosphere united the 'rooms' and the clubs of judges, lords, MPs, Chiefs of Staff and mandarins, and reinforced a shared mentality.

Anglicanism is made more attractive not less by its decision to break from this culture and treat women as equally capable of representing the authority of God and Church. Yet it makes even more anachronistic the idea that the king should be head of the Church through male primogeniture. The praiseworthy efforts of the Church of England to open its positions as well as its heart to justice for women points towards disestablishment and the Church moving towards becoming, like the Church of Scotland, an independently recognised spiritual authority. It is doing so not out of disloyalty but in loyalty to its own calling and in the process the monarchy is losing a vital support.

The Army

The Windsors are a military family. They hunt, shoot and ride: the hobbies of an officer class. Brian Sewell has criticised them for their poor aesthetic and cultural performance. But in the projection of an empire, regiments are more important than orchestras, and it is the regiments that they care about. They collect uniforms not paintings, they command ships, fly planes and helicopters, and are trained to be familiar with military equipment from an early age. At the end of July 1993, the *eight* year old Prince Harry undertook his first official public royal duty. It was to mount a Scimitar tank. He was taken to a German barracks of the Light Dragoons by his mother, Diana is the regiment's colonel-in-chief, and with a scaled down tank commander's helmet fitted to his child's head he rolled the Scimitar through a mock battle scene.[11]

Loyalty to the Queen is the commanding allegiance of the armed and secret services and the Royal Family is as impressed by this as any of us would be. Yet here too, a separation has taken place, although of a different kind from that of the Church of England. Peter Stothard, the editor of *The Times*, has observed that one of the changes to most alter attitudes towards the monarchy has been the coming into positions of responsibility of a generation that never knew conscription, never served in the armed forces, and has not experienced the formative set of loyalties impressed by military training.

Intense personal commitment to royal regimental figure-heads is no obstacle to a modern, professional military. But the network of loyalty this generates has ceased to radiate into the wider, political and commercial society. In seeking to expand its congregation the Church has become less 'official'. The army, by contrast, has modernised itself by becoming more professional and cutting back its size and outreach. In both cases the organic link between royalty, via clergy and military, and the British way of life has been severed. If anything, the Royal Family's military predilections now contribute to its separation from rather than centrality for Britain.

Commonwealth and Cold War: symbolising un-importance.

Mrs Thatcher was contemptuous of the Commonwealth. Her husband despised it, as anyone could see from his gleeful reaction to anti-Commonwealth speeches at the Tory Party Conference. It is said that it is only thanks to the Queen's personal commitment that the Commonwealth exists at all. The Queen enjoys the Commonwealth for obvious reasons, it allows her to walk a larger stage. The British, especially many Tory British, dislike the Commonwealth as a disturbing reminder of things they wish to repress: that the Empire has gone, that underdogs can take their place in the sun, and that they are doing so here at home in Britain's ethnic and black communities. The Commonwealth thus generates disloyal feelings in the bosoms of those who otherwise would seek to profess the greatest loyalty to Queen and flag.

Loss of empire and inadequacy of the Commonwealth can no longer be disguised by the Cold War. After German reunification *The Economist* published a scornful article about France. The French project for a world role was in ruins, it observed. Paris had assumed that Germany would remain crippled by its division and the French could gain by representing West Germany's economic might. But now Germany has become a power in its own right, *The Economist* gleefully observed, leaving France in its shadow. A shrewd assessment but there was an unstated assumption that the end of the Cold War was just a problem for France. In America, from 1989 to today, debate about the role and interests of the US after the collapse of the Soviet bloc has been sustained and serious, if unresolved. In Britain there is almost silence. Yet nowhere has the sudden end of the Cold War been so devastating for the ruling elite's international role.

The British helped to invent the Cold War with Churchill's 'Iron Curtain' speech in 1945. London encouraged confrontation between Moscow and Washington while discouraging an armed conflict that would have flattened it between them. Mrs Thatcher played out this role admirably, 'doing business' with Gorbachev while inciting Reagan to pile Pelion on nuclear Ossa to contain the Soviet threat. The 'special relationship' was an alliance within the NATO alliance, giving Britain a special influence in the confrontation of one super-power with the other. It may have been more important for the UK than for the US, especially so for the intimations of greatness and the memoir reflections of the British diplomatic establishment. Nonetheless, there was an importance. The end of the Cold War has collapsed this inflation definitively.

And the monarchy, our head of state, the 'personification of the nation' in Portillo's phrase, is left personifying Britain's international unimportance. It is difficult to describe the loss of a possible future. One has to imagine things being different to the way they are now. But if the coup against Gorbachev in 1991 had succeeded and a military dictatorship had consolidated power in Moscow, with the aim of reversing the losses of 1989, NATO forces in West Germany would have been reinforced and placed on alert, to convince the Soviet Union of Western resolve. Naturally, Charles and his glorious wife would have visited the troops to raise morale, and they *would* have raised morale. What could the Kremlin have come up with to match Diana? In these circumstances the personal difficulties of their marriage would have remained, but the separation would not have been allowed. The public façade Diana found unbearable would have been borne for a larger purpose.

Today, there is no larger purpose or international interest, imperial, Commonwealth or Cold War, for which the mobilisation of identification is needed and which the Royal Family has uniquely been able to provide. Unless an international catastrophe develops, the Royal Family has been deprived of an important if little acknowledged source of support. As David Hare read out his passionate argument at the Monarchy Conference some in the audience cried 'traitor'. In the absence of international confrontation this accusation carries far less force.

Aristocracy and Economy

The monarchy was truly representative, in some ways modestly, of a hereditary order; imperial overseas and aristocratic, not democratic, at home. Authentic aristocratic influence extends deep into modern times. The last Prime Minister in the House of Lords was the 3rd Marquis of Salisbury who left Downing Street in 1902. But half a century on, his grandson the 5th Marquis was a senior voice in the Cabinet from 1952 to 1957. Some things have changed. Today the House of Lords has been taken over by life peers who are not aristocrats but people who 'got on their bikes' or clung to the greasy pole. Life peerages, indeed, are a neat example of the way the Empire State refashions itself. A modernisation, in that they break with the hereditary principle, they concentrate rather than democratise political power because they increase the Prime Minister's patronage.

As the influence of the hereditary peerage and the relative wealth of the landed aristocracy has declined, the Royal Family has been stranded, like a beached whale caught on the sands of crowd popularity as the tide of its own natural medium withdraws. Part of its problem is that as the other European empires crashed or were overthrown after 1914 the possibilities of marital alliance between royal families were much diminished.

As a result the Royals have been trapped inside a socially incestuous network that is living off even, photographers and equerries, as it implodes. Andrew Morton argues the point convincingly in terms of the marriage between Charles and Diana. They first met when Charles was having an affair with Diana's elder sister. Her middle sister is married to the Queen's private secretary. Her father was an Equerry to George VI and Elizabeth II, her maternal grandmother was, and remains, a Woman of the Bedchamber to the Queen Mother. Indeed, the Spencer children dislike the Queen Mother for obliging their grandmother to give testimony against her own daughter (and their mum) in the divorce court, to ensure that the Earl retained custody of his offspring. If Diana were to have her way and see Charles withdraw from the succession, she herself would become Queen Mother, a suitable reprisal. Meanwhile, the husband of Charles' paramour Camilla Parker-Bowles (herself the descendant of a Royal mistress) is Silver Stick in Waiting to the Queen.[12]

The monarchy has deep wells of support to draw upon. But today it is surrounded by a caricature of aristocracy that isolates it from the world and turns the old dignities of knighthoods and honours into a joke. The farce of 'handles', or 'gongs' like 'Commander of the British Empire' captures and disfigures ambition. As Matthew Parris wrote in *The Times*:

> Royalty in Britain asks us to believe things that are not true: to show deference for which there is no honest basis. Royalty, placed at the apex of aristocracy, legitimises habits of deference to qualities other than merit. Royalty in Britain is the single most potent symbol of class, and all the unfairness and all the waste of human potential that goes with it.[13]

Secrecy and the House of Commons

Most people in Britain would not understand it, if a colleague or friend said 'Please can I talk to you on privy council terms'. The phrase in not in the dictionary, or thesaurus. It isn't a secret. It is simply unwritten. It is one of those unwritten technicalities you either know, or, in the case of most of us, don't know. It means – it would do – secret, confidential, not to be passed on or acted upon.

The Privy Council is the sovereign's secret council, as Christopher Hitchens points out. To be privy to it, is to participate in royal sovereignty. The Cabinet itself is a committee of the Privy Council, its secrecy is not simply a technicality of government but a privilege of the Crown. Government by privy council is incompatible with 'open government'. Yet we have a Minister for Open Government. He is, of course, a Privy Counsellor and argues against a Freedom of Information Act despite overwhelming popular support for such an Act in every social class. This Act would state that information held by public bodies belongs to the public as a right, and officials must show the public good reason if documents are to be withheld from public scrutiny. The inner code, the outer body language, call it what you will, the spirit of a Freedom of Information Act is contrary to the spirit of the Empire State in which sovereignty is to be possessed not shared.

When people feel that secrecy is wrong and they cannot hold powerful officials to account, it is not surprising that the easily exposed Royal Family becomes the victim of the ancient British liberty of a free press. The adversarial noise of parliament drives out real argument, and the party whips most independence of mind in MPs. It is especially symbolic that the logo of the House of Commons is a lowered portcullis: the *closed* gateway through the fortifications of a medieval castle. The defences have been breached elsewhere and the Royal Family are exposed to the lascivious resentment of those who feel wrongly excluded because they cannot cross the moat publicly, enter and share the castle with pride. The cult of secrecy inflames feelings of frustration. Revenge is vented on an isolated and exposed Royal Family. This may make the monarchy a humanly intolerable condition. But privacy laws will not be acceptable if they are privilege laws. The right to personal privacy must be accompanied by the right to freedom of expression and a Freedom of Information Act – the right to know. Rights that in turn demand constitutional codification not royal approval.

The survey could continue. The point has been demonstrated. The monarchy has witnessed a devastating loss of its supporting institutions (Church, Army, Aristocracy) and culture (international importance, official secrecy). The crisis, therefore, lies not in the monarchy but in our country's system. . . and our acceptance of it.

Bagehot's Theory

Having seen how the twentieth century revolution in British society has left the throne so isolated we must also ask *why* this has occurred in this way. What kind of collapse has taken place? It is best to start with the most widely accepted theory of the monarchy, the one developed by Walter Bagehot and published in 1867 in his book *The English Constitution*. Bagehot was a friend of Gladstone and the successful founder of *The Economist*. His arguments were to form the education of Queen Victoria's descendants.

No one thinks we are actually ruled by the Queen. The divine right of kings was destroyed on the battlefield of Naseby three-hundred and fifty years ago. Royal absolutism was first smashed here in England – an enormous liberation for humankind. When we talk about the monarchy what is at issue is not whether a king or queen governs us in a medieval sense. Bagehot applied himself to the question of who rules and how they do so. He concluded that Britain enjoys an *un*-royal form of Cabinet government (his italics), one that is republican, because ruled by the head not the heart, it fuses executive and legislative powers, without checks or balances. Our constitution, for Bagehot, was simple, efficient and proudly 'modern'.[14]

Government, however, has to deal with the 'credulous masses', who are backward. A republic is a state of reason, but, among the people, hearts sway minds. A theatre of appearances is therefore needed, Bagehot argued, to 'excite and preserve the reverence of the population'; to capture people's loyalty and at the same time deflect it, and thus protect the actual machinery of government from popular scrutiny and concern. If you want an image of Bagehot's view of the English Constitution it is that the 'masses' worship and fear the many glittering eyes of the peacock's tail while the banal and tasteless fowl gets on with the job of fattening itself as best it can. Thus monarchy insures obedience and loyalty to the State while behind the throne the efficient, republican machine does the business.

As Tories like Portillo call on us to be true to the nineteenth century, it is fascinating to realise that the central presumption of Bagehot's celebrated nineteenth century view is that the actual government of Britain is republican. This republican core gave Britain, he argued, a *Constitutional* Monarchy. His book is called 'The English Constitution' not 'The English Monarchy'. One of its aims is to show that we have a constitution as good as if not better than America's. In a striking passage Bagehot scorns the notion of Britain's 'so called' checks and balances, and the naïvety of America's constitution makers for believing Britain had them, when it did not:

> The Americans of 1787 thought they were copying the English Constitution, but they were contriving a contrast to it. Just as the American is the type of *composite* Governments, in which the supreme power is divided between many bodies and functionaries, so the English is the type of *simple* Constitutions, in which the ultimate power upon all questions is in the hands of the same persons.[15]

Those persons were not royal. Power belongs to the Prime Minister. The monarch has the right only to be consulted, to encourage or to warn.

There has been much argument over whether the monarch's role has been greater than Bagehot allowed. Such details, as I've suggested, are technical. Bagehot poses two central and truly constitutional questions. First, does Britain *have* a modern, efficient, secret administration? Second, is this something the British people are incapable of overseeing through the ballot box and other mechanisms? Must modern government in these islands proceed in disguise?

Reassessing Bagehot

Bagehot is now under attack. Sir Robert Rhodes James, a historian who was once Clerk to the House of Commons and then an MP seeks to undermine Bagehot's central thesis on the monarchy. He says that the monarch is still an independently powerful element in British government, and the Queen has *not* been reduced to a mere decoration with only a right to warn. We will never know the power Elizabeth II exercises, he argues. This privilege will be left to historians in future generations, just as it is only we who can be aware of how Victoria was far more powerful and interventionist than Bagehot could know in his time. According to Sir Robert, whose lecture to the Royal Society of Arts I had the privilege to chair, this continuing exercise of secret royal power is beneficent. We are fortunate to have it. And the less we know about it the more fortunate Britain will be.[16]

A more plausible criticism of Bagehot is that things have changed but should not have done so. In his recent sweeping survey of the constitution, Ferdinand Mount, editor of the *Times Literary Supplement* and one time policy adviser to Mrs Thatcher in Downing Street, concedes that there has been a 'bold and dramatic simplification of our constitutional arrangements' of the kind observed by Bagehot. He regrets this and enjoys himself assaulting Bagehot's breezy, practical approach, protesting that such pragmatism is not 'the age-old British way of doing things . . . in fact, it has really grown up only during the past 100 years and is a symptom of decadence rather than continuity'.[17]

Only the last 100 years! This is writing with attitude. While Rhodes James holds that monarchy has *always* remained a check and balance on government, Mount says we should *return* to the checks and balances of the eighteenth century, as if the nineteenth was a mistake, 'A little ingenuity, it could be argued, might enable us to repair the damage of the last century or so'. And he welcomes the outburst of royal policy statements by Anne, Charles and others, in 1990, as a return to those earlier times when kings and queens spoke their minds openly and exercised what influence they could.

Mount's attempt to take us forward to the past will require more than 'a little' ingenuity. For what has happened in the last 150 years is not some easily repaired damage, as if just the fabric was torn. The state structures created in Britain during and since the nineteenth century consolidated and preserved an empire. They were not an error of interpretation by madmen and Fabians, as Mount suggests.

There is a third and more fruitful criticism of Bagehot. Proposed by Tom Nairn in *The Enchanted Glass*, it was suggested and then abandoned by Richard Crossman in his introduction to the 1963 paperback edition of Bagehot's book. Crossman was a maverick Labour politician in love with the practicalities of the machinery of government, perhaps as a substitute for his lack of commitment to any principles. In his introduction to *The English Constitution* Crossman describes Bagehot's thesis that behind the glitter of appearances there is a knowing, cynical core of men in charge who run the show. He comments on the implausibility of this and adds:

> Indeed I am tempted to *reverse* Bagehot's stereotype and to assert that the secret of our political stability is the deferential attitude of our rulers [while] scepticism . . . is only to be found among the masses on the sidelines of politics.[18]

There speaks a Labour politician of the old school, confident that the 'masses' (an ugly and patronising term) are safely on the sidelines. Tom Nairn does not resist the temptation. He indeed argues that it is our rulers who are deferential. There is no efficient heart to the English Constitution and what may once have been a modern machine, republican in spirit behind the royal decoration, is no more. Today the decoration has become flesh. The dress and regalia have taken possession of the arms, legs, heart and genitals; the pin-stripes have penetrated the brain; a mutant has been implanted and reproduces itself creating a race apart: the British mandarin. Don't watch the skies – watch out for the honours list. There, twice a year, another cohort is seized by the throat and starts to emit that peculiar sound of throttled self-importance which is the sign of the royal body-snatcher. A few have the inner spirit and energy to resist. For the rest, our *rulers* are the true believers, not Bagehot's pragmatic disbelievers. Credulous and reverential, monarchism not republicanism is the heart of British government.

We have to be careful here. It is easy to mock the British Establishment, especially now that those who once hypnotised the world with their style and achievement have a thirty year record of botching things up. But we should not project this collapse and decline back to the nineteenth century just because their style, elegance and techniques were formed at that time. Until the 1960s British rulers were staggeringly successful compared with countries elsewhere, especially in terms of the admiration and consent they commanded at home. This success within Britain reflected the Empire's global achievement. It was led by what a new study terms 'Gentlemanly Capitalists'.

Gentlemanly Capitalists

In a sustained, two-volume survey of British imperialism from 1688 to 1990, Cain and Hopkins explode the idea that there was a bourgeois conspiracy behind the Empire. They demonstrate that a flexible elite of 'gentlemanly capitalists' dominated British policy and politics. Linked to the aristocracy through land and finance, at ease in banking and the City rather than industry and the regions:

> The men who shaped Britain's imperial destinies were neither representatives of the industrial bourgeoisie nor Olympian figures removed from material concern. With a focus on the monarchy, a spacious world view, and an inventive turn of mind, they fought for their interests with skill and tenacity.[19]

The authors go on to show that it is mistaken to think that imperial Britain was locked into decline from 1914. Twice after the world wars, in 1918 and 1945, it reconstructed a far-flung, international sphere of influence. The gentlemen capitalists would never have called it 'loadsamoney', many of them certainly continued to make it. It is essential to emphasise their success for our understanding of what is happening now. In 1953 Queen Elizabeth was crowned at a moment of achievement and imperial growth (if the last one) as the Pound Sterling once more formed a global zone of wealth banked in the City.

Within three years, however, its decision to invade Egypt and seize the Suez canal forced the Conservative Government to choose between Empire or currency, between pride or the pound. They were capitalists before they were gentlemen, and the end of imperial pretensions followed swiftly. In 1963, de Gaulle refused to allow Britain to enter Europe. The political leaders of the gentlemen capitalists had, for the first time, lost their way completely on the world stage. The crisis began.

Two compensating movements, military and financial, allowed it to be an extended crisis. At the same time as British forces were obliged to withdraw from Egypt in 1956, Soviet tanks successfully reoccupied Hungary. The Cold War became a permanent feature of the continent, and gave Britain a world role. The army was assuaged for the loss of the colonies, it dropped conscription and professionalised itself in readiness to take on a serious enemy. Just as the army found better things to do, so did the City, which embraced the fortunes to be made from the exponential growth in world trade and financial services, symbolised by the Eurodollar. The experience of global empire prepared the City to take off into international financial space, which it did with alacrity, leaving most of the United Kingdom economy behind.[20]

So Bagehot was wrong in a most interesting way. It was not the case that there was a solid, secret group of dull bourgeois running the country while monarchy and aristocracy distracted the public. As Crossman suspected, the administrative class was and is itself in thrall to royal pretensions and participated in them. But this elite was *not* a group of incapable, aristocratic toffs, unable to bring wealth and development to the country. On the contrary, imperial pretention was accompanied by attainment, in war, in trade, in banking and ownership. Right up to 1955 and beyond, tradition was bent to ensure performance. Britain's empire was 'not the result of a conspiracy by a small, covert group who hijacked policy and made it serve their own ends, but the product of a gentlemanly elite whose position was openly acknowledged and widely accepted'.[21] What you saw was what you got. Nobody saw the gentlemen capitalists building British industry and democracy; this was the work of others. But people did see them making Britain great. And they did.

The Empire State

In making Britain great the gentlemanly capitalists created an 'Empire State'. Parts of its institutions were new, like the reformed civil service and local government. Outside the state proper, the public schools and the clubs of Pall Mall formed and protected the culture and behaviour of the political elite of gentlemanly capitalists. The central instruments of the Empire State were remade from traditional material, especially the monarchy and the Palace of Westminster. Everything else – army, church, judiciary, broadcasting, industry and foreign policy – would be subordinated to it.

Domestically, its imperial nature is etched in its instruments of administration. The modern civil service established by the Northcote-Trevelyan reforms was linked to the development of the Indian Civil Service. It laid the basis for an independent and economical administration, with exceptional standards of probity, and promised promotion on merit to those it recruited. But it was not a career open to talent. Recruits had to be suitably male, Oxbridge and clubbable. Behind the device of ministerial accountability, control of the state machine was in the hands of 'Permanent Secretaries' independent of party but also independent of the public, from whose scrutiny they were shielded. A classically educated clerisy, bound by duty to the higher cause of empire managed the show.

In a related way the framework for British 'local' government, as the term suggests, was modelled on the practice of colonial indirect rule, as Jim Bulpitt has shown in *Territory and Power in British Politics*. Politically, an independent minded Conservative, Bulpitt uncovers the mechanisms that gave Britain a cohesive local administration, independent of geographical boundaries, that utilised historic identifications with place and county. Bulpitt distinguishes between 'high' and 'low' politics.[22] The centre, Whitehall and Westminster, in true imperial fashion jealously guarded high politics, such as overall fiscal control, and relations *between* the parts. The locals did not consider policy, whether in energy, transport or housing. Their task was the time consuming 'low' detail of handling the natives face to face.

This is not the place for a full description of the Empire State but I want to emphasise two things. Although it was an Empire State it was not essentially a colonial one. It had a world role before the high period of colonialism in the nineteenth century, and was able to shed the colonies with comparative ease. Second, in giving the ruling system we have inherited a simple name I am not claiming that it had a simple history. Its development was punctuated by great crises. It came close to losing in both world wars. But having won it defaulted back to its imperial formation.

We have inherited, therefore, a living anachronism. Sometimes this is obvious, as with the House of Lords, or the proceedings of the House of Commons, or the absence of a written constitution. Taken singly, each one might seem bizarre or irritating but, we are persuaded by their particular defenders, also basically harmless, hard to change and not worth the enormous fuss of doing so. (It is interesting to note that these same defenders usually praise the flexibility of the system even as they tell us it is almost impossible to reform.) There is thus a strong temptation to scorn and ridicule the way Britain is governed, and there are times now watching television when, so healthy is Britain's comic tradition and so weak its politics, it seems no longer possible to tell when satire ends and reality begins.

Nonetheless I want to take it seriously. The Empire State is systemic, its anachronisms a formidable set of institutions linked by their procedures to each other, which is why reform of any one is so hard. It is an exceptionally concentrated system of sovereignty, whose power is symbolised but not exercised by the monarchy. In its heyday its wonderfully elaborated tentacles of influence and control were feared and admired while economically they delivered. Its success must be our starting point, because today we suffer from its strengths. It is not habits of accent, dress, secrecy, and recruitment from Oxford and Cambridge, that make British government now incongruously imperial in its behaviour. Rather, the fact that these habits continue is a measure of the power of the institutions inherited from the Empire State.

Blaming the Natives

For over thirty years our leaders have sought to solve the problem of Britain's decline with a variety of panaceas: white hot technology (Prime Minister Wilson, 1964); entry into the Common Market (Prime Minister Heath, 1970); the social contract (Prime Minister Wilson 1974); 'Crisis, what crisis?' (Prime Minister Callaghan 1978); monetarism and competition (Prime Minister Thatcher 1979); the Falklands spirit 'Britain found herself again in the South Atlantic and will not look back from the victory she has won' (Prime Minister Thatcher 1982, requoted in her memoirs in 1993). Accompanying this catalogue of dashed hopes there has been a cataract of buck-passing. Our problems have been blamed successively on dead wood in the boardroom, on trade unions, on local councils, on Europe, even single mothers. The latest, and one would wish the last scapegoat, is Michael Portillo's effort simply to blame the critics of our institutions as the cause of our decline.

Those who propose their various solutions, and name-call the rogues gallery of culprits, are *despite themselves* the problem. In awe of the past achievements of the Empire State they presume that, whatever their own shortcomings, at least those in charge of Britain know how to govern. British rulers think the country has a native problem. That the natives are stubborn, have the wrong attitudes, form trade unions or do not know how to run companies, won't work hard, won't invest and won't compete. The truth is that the natives have a ruler problem. We have inherited an Empire State and having lost the empire and entered Europe, we are in urgent need of a non-Empire State.

Why, given their legendary intelligence and skill, has our political class taken as a whole so far failed to reach this simple conclusion? Why has it failed to offer a clear lead to building a new, democratic state for Britain?

In the first place because it was so successful right up until the beginning of the sixties. Full of its own epochal achievement and feeling assured that its grand tradition of flexibility allowed it to adapt to anything, the political class could do nothing other than preserve itself. This was its duty for the country.

Secondly, because the Empire State is a 'Leviathan' that is undemocratic to its heart. It is the impediment to democracy in Britain and cannot be the instrument of its introduction.

Some may regard this allegation as unfair. We have long democratic traditions. The state enjoys exceptional public support, it has a history free of fascism and, except at times in Ireland, its historic use of coercion has been mild by European and American standards. This is so, but it is not democracy – if this is defined as government of the people, by the people, for the people.

The British state *has* been exceptionally concerned to garner and retain popular assent and acceptance. The identification with the Empire, the organisation of welfare when this has been essential, the buying off, heading off and incorporation of dissent, at all this aristocrats and gentlemen capitalists were supremely good. This quality dates back to the formation of Britain in the late eighteenth and early nineteenth century, when, as Linda Colley has shown, widespread fear of the French-Catholic enemy, and identification with the achievements of conquest and colonies, rallied the peoples of England, Wales and Scotland to Britishness.

With a relatively free press, freedom to trade, and a tradition of juries supporting a belief in the independence of the law, the Englishman was freeborn and regarded his country as a land of liberty. But none of this is the same as the rule of the people. Not only was such an outcome resisted. Efforts to forestall it (as we have seen with the creation of the civil service and local government reforms) were perhaps the *driving motive* for the constitutional reforms of the nineteenth century that created the Empire State here at home.

The Great Reform Act of 1832 that abolished rotten boroughs and introduced a formal voting system began the systematic reforms that created the Empire State. Presenting the Bill to the Lords, Lord Grey said 'The principle of my reform is, to prevent the necessity for revolution. . . there is no one more dedicated against annual parliaments, universal suffrage, and the ballot, than I am'. He was supported by his fellow Whig, the historian Macaulay who believed that democracy was 'fatal to the purposes for which government exists'. 'The Whigs aimed', one of the Act's historians writes, 'to *frustrate* democracy by increasing the franchise'.[23] Just as the vote was a device to block democracy, the monarchy was celebrated because, in Bagehot's words, 'The masses of Englishmen are not fit for an elective government'. From 1832 onwards British ruling gentlemen sought to adjust to public demand in order to ensure that their sovereignty remained intact. Consent has been their aim, democracy their enemy.

The Leviathan

At the front of Hobbes's *Leviathan* a seventeenth Century engraver has left us a lasting image of this idea of sovereignty. The giant crowned Leviathan does not crush but absorbs into himself the very bodies and persons of his subjects, who enter his being willingly and provide him with his strength. (I imagine that each time she approved the appointment of 'one of us', Mrs Thatcher felt the body of her sovereignty expand.) It is an image of consent whereby all willingly entrust themselves to one authority:

> Everyone, as well he that Voted for it, as he that Voted against it, shall Authorise all the actions and judgements of that Man or Assembly of men, in the same manner, as if they were his own. . .[24]

Thus they freely defer to and identify themselves with the body of rule, its orb and sceptre. Enoch Powell understood the point, in his famous assessment, 'We are not a democracy we are a Parliamentary nation'. Powell always insisted that sovereignty divided is sovereignty lost. By definition, for him there can be no such thing as shared sovereignty or checks and balances, the authority of the nation may have one body only.

As Enoch Powell's view might be dismissed as doctrinaire pedantry, rather than the wisdom of a practical man, let us turn to the assessment of an ever practical, ever loyal, long-serving Conservative who has collected the highest honours on the way: Lord Hailsham, Lord Chancellor from 1970–74 and 1979–83. He has recently published a classic defence of our form of government, titled *On The Constitution*. He has chapters on the Monarchy, the Executive, the legislature, the cabinet, the party system, the Commons, the Lords, the Church, the judiciary, the armed forces, the police, the civil service, Europe and regional government. Every element of our constitution is included it seems. Indeed, when I opened it I looked at the chapter headings with admiration. Here at last was a systematic defence of the status quo aimed explicitly, Lord Hailsham says, against 'Charter 88, "Bill of Rights" (in the American sense) and the like'.[25]

But something seemed puzzling, an element was surely missing. Could *this* be all that the constitution was about? Then it dawned on me ... The people! Call them the electorate, or the voters, but unlike policemen, soldiers, civil servants and politicians, they do not figure in the ex-Lord Chancellor's understanding of a constitution. Hailsham explains at the start: 'It is no good beginning with ... vain abstractions like "the people" '. Having so decided not to begin with the people, whether abstractly or not, one searches for them in vain through the middle to the end. The voter, the freeborn Englishman, the citizen, the poor subject even, plays no independent part. They are simply ruled.

There is, however, an awareness of individuals when Lord Hailsham finally concedes room for some small improvements:

> there is a need for the political Leviathan to devolve its responsibilities downwards and enlist the funds, the activities, the enthusiasm, and the loyalties of the small platoons. For this purpose it need not sacrifice its ultimate sovereignty, its normative and invigilating responsibilities, its duty to prescribe standards and impose duties.[26]

This perfectly captures, this *is*, the traditional voice of British power and its Empire State. And democratic it is not. If you want your enthusiasm, loyalty, activities and funds to be enlisted, then you know to whom to turn. And it still remains important to understand that it worked. It is obnoxious to be patronised as part of a 'little platoon' in 1994. Little platoons were 'damn good' during the empire, and Lord Hailsham was born into Edwardian England at its height. For all its terrible waste, in war and peacetime, the bottom line came out better than anyone else's.

Then, but no longer. The 'little platoon' mentality, whether on the part of the officer class or in the minds of the people themselves, is no good at all for a modern country in the next century, now just half a decade away.

Consensus and Conviction

At the turn of the nineteenth century, Britain was one of a set of Leviathans, among them Germany, Austro-Hungary, France, Russia. All had imperial regimes seeking to exploit the industrial revolution. By the middle of the century all had fallen – except Russia where Stalinism preserved a form of imperial regime for a further forty years. Britain, like the rest, lost its empire. Uniquely, however, its capital was never captured by insurrection or invasion and the regime itself survived. The question this old regime faced with increasing urgency after 1945 was whether it could turn its reduced circumstances to advantage, in the way that loser nations like Germany and Japan proved able. To achieve this it had to apply itself to internal economic development. Two great attempts followed to bend the British Leviathan to this task, now known respectively as 'consensus' and 'conviction' politics.

'Consensus politics' was the most important example of this process. It was forged by Conservatives and Labour together under Churchill in wartime, and then carried forward into the construction of the full-employment welfare state by Labour after 1945. Consensus politics was thus a cross-party agreement on fundamentals despite the reproduction of adversarial politics in parliament. It played a critical role in the post-war revival of the Empire State.

The freedom that Britain stood for when compared to fascism, the dogged allegiance of British people of all classes once mobilised by Churchill, the financial and material support of empire, made it possible for Britain to resist Nazi domination in 1940. Without this Hitler would not have been overcome. It was Britain's finest hour and a greater confirmation of any regime is hard to imagine. Consensus was built upon it. The British, rulers and peoples together, concurred that there should be no return to the social divisions of the 1930s, that there had to be full-employment if possible and universal provision of basic education, health services and pensions. The consensus that resulted was paternalist. It was in many ways a closed system, riddled with snobbery and easily represented by the monarchy. But it was not weak or 'wet', any more than the monarchy is weak. The people demanded it, they deserved it and they willingly declined to challenge the victorious political system if it would deliver it. The result was 'Churchillism', a complex amalgam that meant different things to different classes, but which was the most popular expression ever of Empire State consciousness.[27]

The Labour Government of 1945 led by Clement Attlee helped to consolidate the spirit of Churchillism. Perhaps its greatest tragedy was that under its influence and the success of wartime organisation, it believed that efficiency was incompatible with democracy. As it nationalised and central-ised welfare, it destroyed the widespread network of volun-tary organisations that Paul Hirst has called associative democracy.[28] Labour's paternalist approach was summed up by Douglas Jay when he became a young Labour minister after 1945: 'The gentleman in Whitehall really does know better what is good for the people than the people know themselves'.

Margaret Thatcher makes much of this remark in the introduction to her memoirs.[29] As someone convinced that *she* knows best, her conviction approach has a final place in the Leviathan tradition. But on one thing she was right. Consensus politics failed. After thirty years, the Attlee settlement finally collapsed in the so-called 'Winter of Discontent' of 1978–79.

Her own failure followed. When the architects of consensus had looked back to the slump and recession of the thirties and the victory of wartime planning they concluded that the market was stupid and wasteful and the state knew best. After consensus politics failed, Thatcher and her supporters reversed the terms. Now the state was stupid and wasteful and the market knew best.[30] Both approaches were products of the Leviathan mentality that knows only one source of authority. Elsewhere, 'developmental states' like Germany with its policy of 'co-determination', have institutions which encourage co-operation. The Empire State is too inhospitable an environ-ment for governance of this kind, which is why a democratic settlement is essential to return prosperity to Britain.

Nonetheless, there was a bracing liberation to the advent of the Thatcher era as toffs were put to the run and stuffy presumptions and closed shop mentality assaulted. It was a populist attempt to replace the old Establishment by one personally approved of by Thatcher herself. Desiring to unlock the energies of 'our island race' and get the state 'off our backs' Thatcher concentrated the powers, traditions and legacy of the Empire State into herself as she drew upon its commitment to 'high' politics. She would open Cabinet meetings saying, 'I haven't much time today, only enough time to explode and have my way'. A caricature of leadership. One of those who eventually felt obliged to resign was Geoffrey Howe, her first Chancellor of the Exchequer. He recalled that:

> For Margaret Thatcher in her final years, there was no distinction to be drawn between person, government, party, and nation. They merged in her mind as one seamless whole. Her interests were axiomatically those of Britain. Any criticism of her was an unpatriotic act.[31]

Louis XIVth, the 'Sun King' had a phrase for this, 'L'état c'est moi'. Whether he actually said it or not, I and many others were taught that he said it, as proof of how much better we were than the French. Already by the seventeenth century, we learnt, if anyone tried to go around our country being absolutist and saying 'I am the State' we chopped off their head. Not that we were against kings, it was understood. We loved having them, only we loved liberty more.

The concentration of power claimed and exercised by Thatcher subverted the ethic of the old unwritten constitution. Do we blame her, or the constitution? As her successor was as weak as she was strong, yet the process of centralisation continued, the answer seems clear. In a recent Charter 88 Sovereignty Lecture delivered in Scotland, Neal Ascherson observed that both 'Thatcherism *and* post-Thatcherism have displayed a striking dialectic: less government means more government. The retreat of the State from the economy has been accompanied by a huge centralising surge in the powers of the State'.[32] Local government has been a tragic victim. The rate of increase in centralisation still accelerates. Quangos, unelected hospital trusts, national curricula being written and re-written, and the creation of so called Henry VIII powers to undo legislation without consulting parliament, are the overt signs. Behind them the covert world of manipulation, the seedy half-truths and arrogance revealed by the Scott Inquiry, allow us to witness the sun of the Empire State collapsing in on itself to form a black hole.

Naturally, as she sucked sovereignty into herself, Margaret Thatcher came into a suppressed conflict with the Queen. Coldness and hostility marked the relationship of the two women. With good reason, if Tom Nairn is right, for he argues that by her assault on consensus Thatcher raised the banner of Englishness against a monarch who is British in every respect. In so doing, he thinks, Thatcher has definitively shattered the enchantment of the monarchy.[33] This may well prove right. But throughout the eighties the two women coexisted. There was no overt conflict because they shared and still share a common assumption about what it means to rule. Born just six months apart, both were formed by and adore the last of the glory days of British power. Mrs Thatcher wanted 'to put the Great back into Britain'. A Churchillist, the Queen preferred to hold on to whatever greatness remained. Both worship Leviathan. Both assume and accept as natural as the day they were born, that power is singular and established, its source unified and known. This was the shared premise, the governing idea behind consensus as well as conviction politics.

Can there be Change?

Britain's Empire State has an integrated constitutional system whose final remaining strength is that it has lasted – lasted longer than any in the world. Naturally, its current practitioners, the occupants and aspirants for its high offices, believe it will continue to do so. Equally, those who have reported on it all their lives and have participated in its unwritten privileges find it hard to conceive of life without it. Together they inform us with all the wisdom of their age and experience that the system will not change.

Yet both consensus and conviction politics drew upon the radical temper of the British spirit, which should not be underestimated. Fundamental reform is possible. Viscount Tonypandy entered the House of Commons as plain George Thomas, a young Labour MP elected in Labour's landslide victory after the Second World War. He was to become one of the most famous Speakers of the House before retiring to his peerage. Reminiscing about his career, he told an interviewer what a deep impression it made on him when he first entered the Commons in 1945 to realise that it ruled 800 million souls.

Today it rules over less than 60 million. When people say that there can't be sweeping constitutional change without a revolution, they forget that there has been a British revolution. The last unchanged structure is the system of authority itself: the Empire State headed by the Queen. Self-assurance is its style, its view that each problem is an exception, a 'local difficulty' in an otherwise untroubled realm. But if difficulties come together. . .

There are at least six forces at work pressing change upon the political system from outside in addition to the forces, such as the Church, at work from within. First, the grievous acts of mis-government that the present system now generates and the anger that this stirs. Second, the growing understanding that such bad government will not be solved by good men or women of any party and the encouragement of such under-standing by dedicated organisations like Charter 88. Third, the growth of internal pluralism, as Britain becomes multi-ethnic and multi-religious society, and minorities claim their rights. Fourth, the resurgence of nationalism, clearly a world force since 1989. The end of the USSR meant the overthrow of Europe's largest multi-national union. The next largest, the UK will not be immune. In 1987, I asked Muscovites about the Ukraine, and the issue was dismissed. The Baltics, yes, but there was no national question between the main neighbours.

Now many fear a war between them. Today, if you ask Londoners about the Scottish question or national feelings in Wales, you are regarded as odd. Ireland, yes, but there isn't really a Scottish question. But there is, and each act of centralisation and abuse of rights by London is magnified by the national injustice in countries that vote against the Conservatives. We *all* inhabit a Union in Britain, a union forged in empire. In the aftermath of the Empire the Union will have to be renegotiated if cohabitation is to continue.

The European Union is the fifth perhaps most important force encouraging internal transformation. If we do not have the wit and confidence to write our own constitution it may impose such a document upon us. Even this last formulation suffers from British defensiveness. To take *our* place in the European Union (and rescue the first person plural from Thatcher) will be to mutual advantage. The United Kingdom, its peoples, traditions and institutions, have much to offer Europe and should help to shape it. This links to a sixth source of change, from capitalism itself whose new forms of organisation encourage initiative, team work and even, as Charles Handy has argued, federalism in larger firms,[34] to ensure that decisions made are carried out effectively. There is a dynamic pull, a call to participate in the re-fashioning of wealth creation in the EU. But as Will Hutton shows, we cannot undertake this within the incubus of the Empire State whose system of sovereignty is incompatible with Europe's.

The Main Parties

Can the political parties advocate the reforms that are needed? The Conservatives are divided on Europe and therefore sovereignty. If ejected by the voters many will embrace what I am going to call the Murdoch variety of constitutional reform, if it will help them back to office. In office their capacity for abandoning the monopoly of power is diminished by the pleasures of the Leviathan. Historically, however, they have been quick to see on which side of the bread there is butter.

Better than their opponents they sense a main chance and thrill to risk. It would be foolish to look only to the current opposition as the agents for bringing down the curtain on the old regime.

The Liberal Democrats have a different problem: they must suffer the injustice of the system. Their call for a new, written constitution is genuinely thought through and far-sighted. Their recent successes in local and shire government means they are now much less of a merely parliamentary party. Especially in England their radicalism has begun to be rooted in interest as well as opinion. However, people feel their's is still the terrible luxury of irrelevance and it does not matter if Paddy Ashdown insists that the system must be transformed when there is apparently no chance that he will run it.

Labour, convinced that it will run the Empire State, has yet to make up its mind about reform. The more the Conservatives centralise power, the more many Labour politicians look forward to it being their turn next. The leadership is committed to a remarkable range of constitutional reforms. But the party is a shrinking violet when it comes to adding them up and saying that a new democratic settlement is needed. An exception can be made of Gordon Brown's Sovereignty Lecture, when he reflected that both the Attlee settlement of 1945 and Thatcher's in 1979 had failed.[35] Britain, he concluded, needs a new constitution for a new century.

The problem here is with the form of words, 'A new constitution for a new century'. The phrase has now entered Labour's policy documents apparently destined for the next election manifesto. But what does it mean? Does it mean a new constitutional settlement, or just a new coat of paint? One source of prevarication lies in the strength of opinion among those MPs and working peers who say 'When we get to power our first task will be to get the economy right, our second to do something about the welfare state and the third may be some constitutional reform such as Freedom of Information'. Their own goodwill convinces them they will do good. Are they oblivious as all hearts sink around them? To take a notable phrase from Neal Ascherson, they have as much chance of opening the way to a prosperous democracy using Britain's existing Empire State as they have getting milk from a vulture.

The parties are part of the problem with the system. If they do not change they too will be victims of the collapse of the Empire State. Can they, indeed, be the instruments for its transformation if this includes electoral reform? Britain's first-past-the-post electoral system is a variant of restricted franchise. In the last four elections the Government failed to win more votes than the Sandinistas did in Nicaragua when the latter were crushingly defeated; while in Britain, Conservative Party 'victories' have given it unchecked sovereignty.

Support for the UK's electoral system often reveals bedrock Empire State consciousness. An example that made a lasting impression on me was provided by Dennis Skinner – a working class Labour MP, legendary for his assaults on royal privilege. I attended a packed fringe meeting at a Labour Party Conference that he addressed. It was organised to defend the existing voting system against 'middle class' electoral reformers. 'I believe in class politics', Skinner roared, and then paused to amplify the effect of his definition of class politics: 'TO THE VICTOR THE SPOILS!' You could almost hear Mrs Thatcher laughing up her sleeve. Skinner believes that class politics means each side gets in order to run things for its benefit. If (to borrow from Ben Okri) the Party of the Rich wins, then the rich gain. If the winner is the Party of the Poor, the poor gain. What could be more democratic than that? But if you think about it, it assumes a royal exercise of state power, one inscribed in the antique character of Skinner's language: 'victor', 'spoils' and so on. He presumes that the purpose of supreme office is to enrich one's family of followers, however these are defined. The aim is constantly to defeat, suppress and put down the other side whose only ambition, like yours, is exclusive power. It is a model of office that is the opposite of democratic. And when you calculate who really benefits from such a system the outcome hardly comes as a surprise.

No one is arguing for a 'year zero'. Necessary reforms take time. However, the reforming spirit of an administration can be discerned instantly the moment it takes office. What is needed is a government well prepared and determined from the start to unlock peoples' energies so as to achieve a pluralist, democratic destination. If we don't get what we need, the forces for change are going to unfold outside party politics to break the constipated, leader-centric constitution of the present Empire State.

Outside party politics, then, there are at least two centres bringing to a focus the different forces for change listed above. One seeks radical but piecemeal reforms without a renewal of constitutional principles, the other calls for an overall resolution and a new popular settlement. The first is vigorously promoted by Rupert Murdoch's News International and parallels the efforts of his coevals abroad such as Italy's media mogul Berlusconi. The second is argued by Charter 88 and others. The Murdoch option favours Americanisation without a constitution. The Charter 88 option is for a democratic constitution that resists Americanisation.

News International or Charter 88

The Murdoch Empire has supported democratic renewal for an empowered individual. The *Sunday Times*, for example, campaigned harder and earlier for a Freedom of Information Act and a Bill of Rights than any other paper in Britain, and it has fought its case at great expense through the courts. The Murdoch media have assaulted the pomposity, paternalism and incompetence of the Establishment with vigour and elan, and gained enormously in the process in the democracy of the market place. This *is* its definition of democracy. The underclass, those who cannot enter the marketplace, are seen as 'not like us', as non-citizens, while the inscription of a set of values for our society as a whole is regarded as antiquated egalitarianism. In a lengthy essay for the *Sunday Times*, Martin Jacques went even further, suggesting that we are witnesses to the end of politics altogether: not just political parties but the likelihood of any attempt at common definitions of our public values in Britain today.[36] All that will exist will be the consequence of social trends and technical change shaped and cashed by monopolies.

The democracy of the marketplace is better than no democracy at all. There is freedom, and some truthfulness despite all the manipulations; a realism and a dynamic that accompanies the concentration and creation of wealth. Strengthened by this, the Murdoch approach seeks to level all impediments to market forces. This does not mean replacing the Queen. *The Sun* needs the monarchy in the way that a bully needs a victim. More important, Murdoch wants a weak state. Public authority can more easily be defied and intimidated if *The Sun* has *more* democratic standing than the Establishment, which it clearly does while the latter is headed by a monarch. Kept in the stocks by *The Sun* so that it can be pilloried at any time, the monarchy has thus become an unwitting partner in the Murdoch project – an agent in the destruction of the values it most cherishes because it can no longer credibly defend them. The thugishness and brutal radicalism of *The Sun* do not just hold the Establishment in contempt. Its scorn for the British public is even greater as it claims that the British people are simply not up to the job of reform. Privatised freedom, high standards for those with cash, an international republic of satellite dishes stamped with the Queen's Award for Exports, this is the market democracy of Murdoch.

Asked if he wanted to see an end to the monarchy, Murdoch replied 'I'm ambivalent about that. I think you'd have to say No, because I don't think the country has the self-confidence to live without it. But is the system holding the country back in this new competitive, open, global village. . Is it inhibiting the country's growth? I think it's debatable'.[37] This reply can be read as a threat. Provided the monarchy does not stand in the way of open, global competition (ie News International) then it can continue. But this will simply reinforce the country's lack of self-confidence. And we really would be lacking in self-confidence if we failed to observe that this lack of self-confidence is no bad thing for Rupert Murdoch and he has no interest in a new constitutional settlement that could address and resolve it.

Towards a New Settlement

Charter 88 wants a self-confident country. The first step is to replace the 'absolute sovereignty of parliament', now a tired formula for incapable administrative dictatorship that few believe in, with a rights based democracy and a constitution in which all can take pride. This would alter the role of our head of state. The Charter's view is that there should be a referendum to decide what type people want. In that order: a new constitution first, then decide the head of state. Shirley Williams calls for a citizens' monarchy. The option is not available within the Empire State to be engineered by Buckingham Palace or a Royal Commission on Democracy. The people have to be citizens first for the monarchy to join them.

Existing opinion means the vote would be for retaining the House of Windsor in the European manner. But the coronation oath would be transformed into a pledge of loyalty to the constitution rather than to bishops. Similarly, the loyalty of our civil servants, police and armed forces would be given to the constitution not the Crown. The throne would belong to us, rather than us belonging to it. Some argue that only with such a constitutional revolution will it possible for a monarchy to escape an otherwise unendurable fate as the plaything of News International.

Charter 88's demands open up a much broader and novel debate on the contents of a constitution. Britain may be holding a hidden asset. Thanks to the longevity of its ancient settlement a new constitution can be formulated after the restrictions of Cold War have lifted. The Cold War helped to perpetuate 'national security states' in the West. Strong central government was needed to defend freedom. Crude representative democracy ensured it. Government was placed in the hands of leaders who had the task of protecting liberty, especially market freedom. If the alternative was dictatorship, the choice was clear, and the democratic legitimacy of Western institutions assured. But the collapse of the Soviet empire did not just free its inhabitants to aspire to become like us. It also frees us from the threat of being forced to become like them. So the end of the Cold War has given us the opportunity, and earned us the right, to ask 'Is this all?' about our own societies. It has accelerated a general crisis in traditional representative democracy, one intensified by advances in education and communications that has put the old party system into question everywhere.

The monarchy debate was one of a series of Charter 88 conventions and lectures that focus on these and other questions about democracy and give a joint platform to the proposals being developed across the spectrum, from the free-market European Policy Forum to the left-leaning IPPR.[38] Questions of representing difference, of equality, of whether democracy can work for women, of the relationship between constitutions and the economy, of the use of referenda and new forms of participation are being explored. The first volume of the *Democratic Audit* will soon be published in an attempt to establish a comparative measurement of the quality of political life in the UK.[39] At the same time some brave Charter supporters have started to canvass door to door to ask people what they think about the constitution.

Two warnings must be attached. The clearer and shorter a constitution the better. It should enhance and empower people and public bodies and not be a substitute for legislation that ought to belong to the republic of argument and votes. A constitution is not an alternative to or a substitute for politics. Many on the left opposed a Bill of Rights because it will give power to judges. Now obliged to support a Bill of Rights they want an entire programme of economic and social issues to be 'entrenched' and supervised by the courts, thinking this is where power will be. Empire State style, they still presume there can be only one location of sovereignty, whereas a democratic constitution puts an end to absolute power anywhere. Nor, therefore, are written constitutions themselves all-powerful instruments. To hear traditionalists talking, you would think a new constitution meant that our Leviathan will be pinned helpless to the ground – not replaced. The point needs emphasis. A constitution is a living thing. A written settlement can only aspire to belong to society as a whole. It will be contested, negotiated and renegotiated as society changes. It is a different way of being different together.

Which leads to the final warning about the call for a democratic constitution. Most of those of liberal, elite opinion in Britain probably want one. But formed by the paternalist tradition of the Empire State, they fear the people; they want to see popular consent, but not control over the way things are run. The Murdoch approach, on the other hand, which now finds recruits within the wealthier Tory ranks, knows how to inflame opinion, raise the Union Jack, and mobilise assent. It may do so on a short-term basis, but it is the master of the short-term. It lives for power now, the devil can take the rest. In terms of intellectual influence, a new overall settlement is likely to win favour. In terms of power, its victory is much less assured; the decisive factor will be the depth and breadth of popular support.

Conclusion

The Monarchy Conference ended with a short, well delivered speech from Lord Rees Mogg in defence of the monarchy. Later, in his column in *The Times*, he concluded that royalists can sleep easily in their beds because the temper of the debate was too reasoned for there to be a threat. This exposes a clear difference of view. The key issue is not the royals it is the system, what I have called the Empire State. Hooked on centralised, absolute sovereignty it gets its fix from black and white confrontations. Its presumption that 'winner takes all' is fed by and feeds the media, who above all want a spectacle. They want glassy eyed republicans calling for aristocrats to be beheaded; they want a war between cavaliers and roundheads; they want a drama that sells papers. The Monarchy

Conference and I hope this book are not part of such a spectacle but part of the solution.

What needs to be solved is the constitutional crisis. The monarchy's is only an expression of it. In a historic country the crisis has historic roots. In its heyday each part of the Empire State's constitution had its qualities. Individuals had the privilege of considerable liberties and toleration, but not the right to them. There were no checks and balances, but consent was regarded as vital even when sovereignty itself was absolutely guarded. Its aspirations can be summed up in two words: world power. The system was not a mystery. The gentlemanly capitalists who created the Empire State governed publicly. So far as the monarchy was concerned, it was not a misleading decoration but a truthful expression of the constitution, at once imperial abroad and based upon loyalty at home. It worked because it was a brilliantly economical way for a modestly sized country to run a world empire.

Today our rights are exposed to arbitrary abolition (the historic presumption of innocence disappeared without serious discussion to please a tricky Conservative Party conference) and are now protected only by a European Court. Powers are being increasingly concentrated, it is not just local government that is being virtually abolished, most countervailing centres to cabinet policy are being broken. As for aspirations, what are our aspirations as a country?

I began by saying that we live under a spell in which we are obsessed with the monarchy but cannot speak of the system by which we are ruled. The Empire State itself has ruled this silence. Denial is its watchword; 'If it's not broke don't fix it' its mantra.

All constitutions are lived. The British State now tries to deprive us of political life, to keep us as subjects by persuading us that we are its customers. It uses the monarchy as a decoy and depends on our silence to survive.

It is time to end the silence. The Empire State *was* brilliant at adapting to new circumstances when the aim was to preserve or enhance itself. The long shadows of a successful past continue to convince those who operate within them that they alone see the light. The rest of us know they are fumbling in the dark. Their regime cannot share power when it is designed to retain power. It cannot successfully adapt to becoming what it is not. With its unitary conception of sovereignty it is a helpless misfit in Europe and a corrupt cripple in Britain, draining away our democratic lifeblood. What was good for empire has become good for nothing.

The Empire State is not a matter of history. It is Britain's constitution. Immensely powerful and successful in its time, its time is up. The source of 'the British disease' is not some vague entity called 'The Establishment', or deference, or an obsession with the countryside and dislike of industry. Such charges may be partially true, if so they are the consequence of an enemy that is not hot air, or cultural weakness, or snobbishness, or the monarchy. It is a machinery of rule, a machinery that governs the way we are governed.

This is why we need a new constitutional settlement: to release us from the Empire State, to allow us to give voice to suitable aspirations, ambitious for us as a people and not self-denigrating or filled with a sense of loss and humiliation. Constitutional reform for Britain is not just a liberal preoccupation or a pleasant idea if only we could have it like clean air. It is as tough and practical a necessity as anyone could wish.

CHARLES MOORE

THE IMPORTANCE OF THE MONARCHY

MY ARGUMENT IS about the importance of the monarchy, rather than a discussion of monarchy in general. I would not want to argue for monarchy in principle. It is a form of government which, to say the least of it, has a chequered history, and which would probably fail if introduced into most countries in the world today. Indeed, I would not want to argue for any form of government in principle. Forms of government arise from the history of nations, from the particular experience of different peoples. They are not universally applicable. It is true that ideas about what government is, or should be, extend beyond national boundaries. They are shared among entire civilisations and, particularly nowadays, are discussed throughout the world. But broadly speaking, the only truth is that nothing in politics is always and everywhere true. The imposition of democracy on a country can just as easily do harm as the imposition of martial law. The real circumstances are what matter. So I base my argument on a premise which I suspect that few in Charter 88 share – that there is no such thing as a universal human right and no ideal form of government for mankind. Government is simply the type of arrangements that societies make, in particular times and places, to run themselves.

Consequently I propose only to explain why I think the monarchy is important for this particular place, Britain, and for this particular time, now.

The most obvious sense in which the monarchy is important to us is that it exists. It is there. The evidence of it is all about us.

It is visible on postage stamps and letter boxes and in toasts at formal dinners. Every day at the tube station I shove two pictures of the monarch into a slot and the machine, which knows nothing about what 'D.G. Reg. F.D.' might mean, and cannot translate *Decus et Tutamen* or *Honi soit qui mal y pense* nevertheless accepts them – at least sometimes – and gives me a ticket in return. That is an epitome of the way monarchy works in our society. It is generally accepted in a day-to-day sort of way, without having to think about it very much. All the elements are in place. We know who the monarch is, who her heir is, and who his heir is. We know what her duties are, how the law circumscribes her and what the constitution expects of her. We know who will open Parliament and receive foreign heads of state and lay a wreath at the Cenotaph and before whom the Colour will be Trooped. These are not merely ceremonial roles. They represent long-standing agreements about things which people often find it very difficult to agree upon, things about which people frequently kill one another. When there is the threat of a coup in many African or Latin American countries, for example, everyone asks whose side the army will be on. In Britain we know the answer to that question: the army is loyal to the monarch, and that's the end of the subject. That is an important reason why we do not have a coup. The question was settled a long time ago and most people are happy to abide by the result.

It is customary to say that one welcomes the chance to have a free and open debate. In this case I would not be honest if I said that I do. In a way, I regret this debate. For the way agreement on the monarch has been long settled is important. By digging it all up again, one is doing something which may be interesting, but is certainly dangerous. The brochure for Charter 88's monarchy debate congratulated itself on the end of what it called 'throat-stopping deference'. But it is a mistake to assume that deference is always stupid or cowardly. It can arise from a proper understanding of the importance and depth of something. One defers, for example, to the grief of a widow or the knowledge of a learned man. One does not shout in church. If deference had stopped the throats of the journalists who dug up the private unhappiness of the royal couples in order to increase their papers' circulations I should have been only too pleased. One ought to defer to the British monarchy – not out of slavish adulation of the individuals involved, but because it contributed so much to the peace and freedom which, on the whole, we still enjoy. The Charter 88 debate on the monarchy took place in the Queen Elizabeth II Conference Centre. It argued over whether we need Queen Elizabeth II at all. If it had been held in the Adolf Hitler Conference Centre, we would not have been free to discuss whether we needed Adolf Hitler. We should be more grateful for this fact than I think most of the contributors to this book are today.

If, like Everest, the monarchy is important 'because it's there', the onus of proof lies heavily on the abolitionists. It is not nearly enough for them to point out current deficiencies. They must also explain what they would put in its stead. And the most important question they must answer is not, how precisely would you organise your new system? Would you have a federal or a unitary state? Would you have a president for life or for a set term? Would he be directly elected and so on and so forth? The vital question is, How on earth would you get people to agree to whatever your plan was? And by 'agree', I do not mean, agree to take part in a vote or whatever. I mean really accept the legitimacy of the new arrangements, really believe – once Buckingham Palace is closed down and the Crown is torn off every public building and a new head is on the coins and soldiers are swearing allegiance to someone else and all the royal societies and royal academies and Royal Tunbridge Wellses have disappeared and *The Times* has a different coat of arms on its front page and a new national anthem has been composed by Sir Andrew Lloyd Webber – really believe that the new people in power have a genuine authority under which one is prepared to live and for which one is prepared to die.

The republican is not, as it were, building with popular approval on a green-field site. He has first to get permission to demolish an old, complicated and much-loved building. Then he has to design a new edifice which will fit in with the existing environment. Then he has to build it, and when he tries to do so he may well find his attempts to get planning consent frustrated at every turn. The new British Constitution could so easily become a political version of the new British Library – expensive, unnecessary, unpopular, ugly, slow to come into use and out-of-date before it is even constructed.

It seems to me that the reformers have hardly begun to think about any of this. They exhibit that particular frivolity which characterises a certain sort of clever person, the pernicious quality that Michael Oakeshott called rationalism. It is the vanity of thinking that your own brainwave surpasses the wisdom of the ages. Inventing a new British Constitution is like inventing Esperanto: it notices all the things which are rich and strange and subtle and cuts them out in order to make something which is of no use to anyone whatever but gives a certain preening satisfaction to its authors.

It is surely obvious that there is no consent in this country for an alternative form of government. There is not even the basis for arriving at such a consent. It seems to me almost literally insane to try to undermine the existing consent in the vague belief that something more modern and egalitarian can be put in its place.

All the arguments I have put so far are not specifically about the monarchy. They are about the danger of disturbing what exists and what, more or less, works.

Let me briefly argue for the monarchy itself.

My first point is simply to deny the claim that the monarchy makes Britain a rigid, stratified, hierarchical society. How does it do so?

If the Queen dies tomorrow her son will kiss hands with the son of an unsuccessful trapeze artist from Brixton and will have the Crown put on his head by the son of a hospital porter from Dagenham. He may, it is true, tend to shoot with people whose families have had many acres for many years, but I do not see how this makes life difficult for the great majority of us who lack those acres. If you say, 'Pull it all down: get rid of distinctions of wealth and rank', I say, 'You are motivated more by resentment than by love of your fellow men'. If you say it all perpetuates snobbery, I reply that if you think snobbery will disappear with the abolition of the institution, you have obviously never been to France or, indeed, to any other country on earth.

My second point is more positive. It is that the monarchy does so many good things which it would be very hard for anyone else to do. For example, it does rather silly, touching or peculiar things very well – like bestowing honours, or holding a garden party or distributing Maundy money or dressing up in funny uniforms and reciting funny words. On the whole, people like these things. They appeal to their imagination and sense of humour and sense of occasion and sense of history. The realm of poetry and fancy is an important part of the life of any nation and it is no accident that one calls it a realm, rather than a republic. A monarchy is an idea for the heart as well as the head, and no alternative satisfies both so well. If you believe, as I do, that it is vital for people to study the history of their country, the best, simplest way to begin is to learn about its kings and queens. The personal principle is a civilised one, but it can easily be corrupted – as in totalitarian leadership cults – or neglected – as in bureaucracies. It is successfully embodied in our monarchy.

Our monarchy also represents another principle which is more and more neglected in modern society, and that is altruism and duty. The Queen symbolically stands for power, which is why she holds the sceptre, but in practice she represents the voluntary laying aside of power – the quality of mercy. She spends a huge part of her life giving attention to all those who try to help other people – visiting schools and hospitals and churches and old people's homes and youth ventures, being the patron of charities, and giving her blessing to good works. And she is seen to be doing this, not in order to aggrandise herself and become more famous and powerful, but simply to uphold what is kind and gentle. The idea of being disinterested is now so rare that many people do not know the true meaning of the word. It applies to the monarch, and it is hard to imagine it applying half so strongly to anyone else.

Let me end with a protest. Many people are concerned, I am sure, about democratic accountability. Many are also concerned for national independence. What an absurd distraction it is to worry about the minor shortcomings of our monarchy when both of these are severely threatened. By far the biggest present assault on our rights comes not from the Crown of the House of Windsor but from the strong diadem of European Union.

SHIRLEY WILLIAMS

A CITIZEN MONARCHY

IN THE PAST, at least, the monarchy helped us to define who and what we are. As a country we are often seen from abroad in terms of the monarchy. It is one of the best known features of this country. In the last 40 years we have lost an empire, struggled to find a new role in the world and finally opted for the Maastricht treaty and the European Union. We have changed our economic structures, we have changed our social structures, and we have changed our educational system. The scale and scope of the change this country has gone through almost amounts to a revolution.

Yet the one thing that has changed very little, save for the pressures of the last few years, has been the monarchy. The Royal Family's way of life, their homes, their houses, the pomp and circumstance that surround them, their court and the procedures by which peers and knights are made, are all unchanged. The monarchy has been a strange island of continuity in the midst of a sea of turbulence. The crucial question is therefore whether the monarchy itself can now change.

My thesis is straightforward. I believe that the monarchy can change, and that it can be of very great value to this country. I believe that if it is unable to change then it will go, as other monarchies have done, the way of history and destruction.

First then, continuity. Continuity is perhaps one of the

most striking characteristics of the United Kingdom. Remember Shakespeare's description of the monarchy and of Britain. 'This royal throne of kings, this sceptred isle, this fortress built by nature for herself against infection and the hand of war.' Such British exceptionalism is a very strong part of our history.

The monarchy has been one of the institutions that have held together the separate parts of the United Kingdom. It has also been, with the short exception of the civil war, an institution that the British people have accepted. Ours is not a revolutionary country, and it is interesting that we have turned back to the monarchy whenever we have been through a period of extraordinary turbulence. And finally, at least until recently, the monarchy has stood for the values of public service, and to some extent family values. The Royal Family has been a living example of the way in which altruism and service to others must be placed ahead of selfishness. In addition there have been a number of constitutional changes to the monarchy of which many of us are unaware.

In 1688 the Act of Settlement established a constitutional structure of checks and balances between three almost equally powerful institutions in Britain: the monarchy, the House of Lords and the House of Commons. But in the two centuries that followed, those checks and balances have basically disappeared. At the time of the Act of Settlement ministers were not responsible to Parliament. They were responsible to the King. The royal prerogative was real.

In the last 200 years the monarchy and the House of Lords have both lost most of their power to the House of Commons. Britain has become a country ruled by one institution. But let us not deceive ourselves. The House of Commons is itself an institution that has allowed its power almost entirely to pass back to the executive, the government, which in this country usually means the government of one party. The executive in Britain has something very close to absolute power, it hides behind the Crown as a way of hiding from us the extent of that power. The Royal Prerogative is now exercised by the Prime Minister.

The executive in this country exercises huge powers of patronage. Who appoints the governors of schools and the members of health boards? It is not the Queen, although it may be done in her name. It is almost invariably ministers of the majority party in the House of Commons.

In my view, our democracy is being undermined by the extent of executive patronage, badly drafted legislation, the huge powers given to bureaucracy and statutory instruments which are no longer adequately scrutinised – where they are scrutinised at all.

One influential concept of the Crown at the heart of the constitution comes from Sir Robert Armstrong (now Lord), speaking in 1982 as the head of the civil service. 'The civil service', he said, 'has no constitutional personality or responsibility, separate from the duly elected government of the day'. In other words, Armstrong defined the responsibility of the civil service to the Crown as responsibility to the government of the day.

Sir Ian Bancroft (now Lord), the previous head of the civil service, had another interpretation. It is one that I find much more attractive. 'The civil service belongs', he said, 'neither to the politicians nor to officials but to the Crown and to the nation'. Sir Ian Bancroft clearly did not regard the government of the day and the Crown as identical. He felt the nation and the Crown were identical and that, I believe, is an important constitutional distinction to make. Prince Philip can be quoted in support of this argument. He said in 1981: 'Once a determined government begins the process of eroding human rights and liberties, always with the very best possible intentions, it is difficult for individuals or for individual groups to stand against it'.

I happen to believe that the monarchy can be an important means of protecting our liberties, though in my view it would require a different kind of monarchy to the one we now have.

The Royal Family has made an attempt to change but I believe it has gone in the wrong direction. It has become soap opera. All of us look at the Royal Family, read the sensational stories in the tabloids as if we were reading about a bunch of film stars. This undervalues what the monarchy can be and can do. The Royals themselves have paid a terrible price for becoming stars on a stage which was not made for this purpose: they now have no privacy and no life of their own.

I am in favour of extending media freedoms, not curtailing them, but if I ever were to take any steps to restrain the freedom of the press, it would be because I also believe the intrusions made into the private lives of many people, including the Royal Family, have become intolerable. We really do have to limit the use of 50-inch camera lenses and bugging devices.

The transformation of the Royal Family into soap opera has also exacted a terrible price from the rest of us because it has reaffirmed what we were and distracted us from what we might be. Looking at my country, what I find most troubling thing is our devotion to the past and our extraordinary unwillingness to think about the future.

Let me conclude with what the role of the monarchy might be. I believe it is possible to have a citizen monarch. I believe this because the Royal Family has shown itself capable of moving with the times. An outstanding example is the willingness of the Royal Family to adapt its role vis-à-vis the Commonwealth. Once the monarch stood at the centre of empire. Today the Queen is the head of state of a widespread international multi-racial grouping which includes people at many levels of economic development.

The Queen has handled that change magnificently. She also deserves much more credit than she has been given for the way in which Rhodesia finally turned into Zambia and Zimbabwe and for the way in which she has stood, with her son the Prince of Wales, for multi-racialism to an extent that, frankly, shames most of our political class. This is one of the finest things that the monarchy has done for Britain.

But why have a citizen monarchy? Why not become a republic? Let's look at King Juan Carlos of Spain. He underpinned the democracy of Spain against the pretensions of would-be dictators. Let's recall the attempted coup against the Spanish Parliament, the Cortez. King Juan Carlos refused to support that coup and thereby helped sustain Spain's multi-party democracy. If Belgium is still one country today, it is because King Baudouin sat at the centre of that country holding the Walloons and the Flemings together. Looking at Europe today we can all see that is not an easy thing to do.

Consequently, I believe there is a role for a monarchy. It is to consult, advise and warn, to embody in institutional form the constitutional traditions and democratic values of the country. Its role in Britain is peculiarly important, for two reasons: first, because the constitution is unwritten, and depends on practice and precedent, second, because executive power rests in part on the use of the Royal Prerogative. Therefore the British monarch has a specific interest, not in using the Prerogative directly, but in ensuring that it is properly and responsibly used by ministers in the monarch's name. This role seems to me both appropriate and necessary, as executive power encroaches on both legislative power and customary limits on its use.

If the monarchy were also to take up the role of guardian of our liberties, by insisting on the proper use of the Prerogative, it could only do so by representing public opinion, since it has no autonomous power. That in turn suggests a different sort of monarchy closer to the people, with a much smaller Court, one that dissociates itself from the pomp and circumstance that now surrounds it. It has to be a less magical monarchy, a monarchy that belongs to the real world. At a time when hierarchy is being challenged, class boundaries are shifting, and feudal patterns of deference are breaking down, such a monarchy would be more secure, able to embody both continuity and change. Such a monarchy might concentrate our minds less on its own future, and more on that troubling aspect of our historic legacy: a powerful executive that is checked neither by a constitution, nor by a bill of rights, nor by a truly independent Parliament.

STEPHEN HASELER

MONARCHY IS FEUDAL

THE PRESENT HIGHLY-publicised personal tragedies and inadequacies of the Royal Family are not the cause of the British monarchy's crisis. Rather, they serve as a catalyst for the long-suppressed discussion and debate about the contemporary relevance of this archaic institution.

This debate has indeed been a long time coming, and for that very reason is now breaking out with a force and suddenness which, to some, is surprising. Yet, for us republicans the surprise lies not in how swiftly the taboo on discussion of monarchy has been exorcised, but rather in the resilience – way into the modern age – of this most anachronistic of our institutions.

After all, monarchy is a feudal institution co-existing uneasily with a democratic age. And although it has managed to survive in Britain into the late twentieth century, most of its props have now been removed – one by one.

Let us start with empire. The last time Britain's monarchy got into trouble – in the 1870s – the country's courtier class (led by Benjamin Disraeli) – decided that the only way it could be revived was by associating the Crown (and the person of Queen Victoria) with the imperial instinct of the late nineteenth century British: and the lavish, pompous, ceremonial monarchy was born. Today's beleaguered royals have no such escape route. Britain's empire, if not her pretensions, died amidst the battles of the Second World War; and the country and its monarchy, could not find a realistic role in the post-war world. Of course, Elizabeth Windsor, in a pale imitation of

Victoria's strategy, attempted to set the Crown on a new, modern, multi-national course by associating it with the rickety Commonwealth of Nations. Yet, this strategy can only end in tears – as one of the major Commonwealth states, Australia, moves towards becoming a republic, an innovation which will certainly affect the future constitutional role of Canada.

As the 'imperial monarchy' became increasingly untenable, royalists came up with the notion of a 'family monarchy' as a way of reconciling the institution with democracy. The idea was that the British public would become enchanted – indeed entranced – by the ambiguity of a group of 'royals' who were, at the same time, both magically different from ordinary mortals and yet similar (a 'mere family'). This manipulative strategy of creating an idealised Royal Family – which would set standards for 'subjects' keen to have examples set for them – worked wonders for George VI and, for a time, for the young Elizabeth II. It was, however, a high risk strategy and has now back-fired amidst the collapsing marriages and irresponsibilities of the real royal clan.

While the 'imperial' and 'family' monarchy is collapsing, other forces are eroding the legitimacy of its associated *ancien régime*.

Perhaps the most profound is the slow weakening, year-on-year, of Britain's remarkable culture of deference. No longer do the British media (certainly not the tabloid press, although the broadsheets and television are a little more reticent) feel a strange need to suspend judgement when it comes to the Royal Family. And, indeed, when judged by normal standards – by, for instance, routine notions of value for money – the whole royal set-up appears egregiously expensive and culturally ludicrous.

Yet, though crucial, the end of deference is an inchoate process, and the monarchy can certainly make its accommodations with a more confident and assertive public possessed of a renewed interest in citizenship – at least for a while.

What must be much more troubling for the Windsor circle – because it is more specific and institutional – is the danger posed by the new European Union. This new Europe works its will against the House of Windsor on two levels. First, by creating for the British a new European citizenship (to replace our present subjecthood), the new union essentially creates a system of dual loyalties. In one fell swoop the modern Briton, should he or she wish, can constitutionally and legally – escape from the confining boundaries of the British royal state and exercise rights of citizenship through European institutions and loyalties.

Perhaps even more importantly the new European Union marks an end to a whole phase of British history. For most of this century we have been unsure of our place in the world and hence defensive about the subject. Are we one nation or many? Are we white, or of many colours? Are we C of E or multi-denominational? Or secular? And we still do not seem able to disentangle ourselves from the identity created by the imperial past, a hold-over which can help explain why we retain, in the face of all the evidence, so many myths about our importance and centrality in the world. In this dispiriting phase of development we have tended to rest upon laurels won centuries ago, upon past glories and, inevitably, upon the seeming security of an historic monarchy. And the Crown re-inforced this culture of backward-looking nostalgia and also, in the process, helped to create a national elite: overly suspicious of change, ill at ease with the virtues and values of business and technology, unfit to compete properly in an increasingly competitive world.

Britain's entry into the new European Union can be a break-point with this dismal past. Constitutionally and legally it is redolent with possibilities, as, arguably, it provides us with the sought-after new constitutional settlement – the kind of constitution which Charter 88 has been pressing for in Britain. Not only does the new constitution of Britain in Europe dispense with the hereditary principle – there is no role for hereditary institutions in the central mechanisms of the Union – but it also introduces the concept (and the reality) of 'citizenship' to our shores. Every Briton, including the Queen herself, becomes a citizen of the new Europe with attendant rights and responsibilities. Most importantly of all, the new union injects into the moribund British body-politic a sense of institutional pluralism, diversity and competition – a spirit of governance which the deadening centralisation of the culture of monarchy has, until now, helped to suppress.

Yet the challenge for us is to finish the job of constitutional modernisation for ourselves. Indeed, it would be a sad irony should the country which gave the world the Magna Carta, the first commercial republic and modern liberalism, also become the country that is stuck with a monarchy well into the twenty-first century.

Those who believe that we British can never modernise our constitution – certainly can never seriously enact a dis-establishment of the monarchy – point to the question of transition (from monarchy to republic) as the insuperable problem. They suggest that even if a republic were the best possible modern system of government, we British cannot live under its blessings because creating such a republic would be too traumatic an experience, the game not worth the candle. Professor Hennessy has argued that so intertwined are the processes of government with the monarchy that it would be almost impossible to unpick them. Thus, so the argument runs, we are for historical reasons lumbered with an hereditary head of state. And thus, instead of attempting to replace it with a different system, we should reform the institution (along Scandinavian lines).

Yet, two factors now conspire to render this typical piece of twentieth century British fatalism redundant. First, the idea that the transition would be traumatic will be put to rest by the experience of Australia as it replaces its monarchy with a republic. This 'Aussie factor' in British politics should not be discounted: for, as an Australian president takes over from the Queen (probably sometime very early in the next decade), the fact that the sky will not fall in and psychosomatic diseases not break out will simply prove the republican point. Army officers, judges and parliamentarians will no longer take an oath to the Queen, but neither social and economic break-down, nor a *coup d'etat* will follow.

A mature society can indeed progress from A (having a seemingly entrenched monarchy) to B (establishing a republic) calmly, intelligently, and without the whole system becoming destabilised.

Secondly, there is the issue of the succession. The fact is that the trauma of becoming a republic looks as though it may be much less intense than the trauma of a new reign: that of Charles III. Elizabeth Windsor cannot go on forever, and, by the time she either abdicates or dies it is inconceivable that a new reign can begin smoothly. When the Queen came to the throne she enjoyed near universal support. Yet when Charles (or, should the House of Windsor attempt to skip a genera-tion, William) 'ascends', the nation will be divided. The Crown, rather than being a part of a constitutional con-sensus, will have become a subject for debate. Monarchy – because it possesses little legitimacy in a democratic age – is at best a fragile institution and its renewal (in the form of a new reign) cannot be substantiated in the cold analytic light of argument.

The end of Elizabeth's reign will, therefore, become the occasion for the British making formal what is already informal, to make official what is already a reality – by turning the republican political virtues in which we all believe into a real republican constitution.

My own view is that a new republican constitution could be enacted quite simply: by an Act of Parliament designating the Speaker of the House of Commons as the head of state. Such a simple bill could be introduced and the Queen, as is now the custom, would agree to sign it.

Such a simple Act of Parliament would, of course, not address the growing concerns of many constitutional re-formers who would want to see the end of the monarchy as the occasion for a wholesale reform package – including a written constitution and a bill of rights, and the disestablishment of the Church of England. Of course, the 'simple bill' option would ignore these fundamental structural defects in the governance of Britain, yet it would be a very valuable start. For the fact is that once the apex of the *ancien régime* constitution is removed

69

then everything else falls quickly into place, and the real constitutional debate can begin.

Of course, some argue that it is inconceivable that Parliament – composed as it is of party politicians – could even contemplate introducing let alone passing such a bill. Politicians, so the argument runs, are so fearful of losing votes on this issue that none of the three parties will ever raise it. This analysis is flawed. First, it takes no account of the rapidly changing public mood on the monarchy – one already sensed by Jack Straw for the Labour party. Certainly, republicanism is not yet a majority sentiment (although it is now supported by something like 20% of the population, many of them in the higher income groups). However, the devastating news for the monarchy is that a vast majority of British voters do not see it lasting for long into the twenty-first century, and around a half of the population now believe that it would make no difference to their lives should the monarchy be disestablished. Secondly, pro-monarchist sentiment (often visceral) is mainly confined to an older generation. However, this generation will not only reduce over time but is the most appalled by the breakdown in the family monarchy and in the traditional standards which it supposed the Windsors stood for.

So, over time, it will become easier (indeed, maybe even popular) for politicians to advocate the replacement of the monarchy by a republic. Even so, the best and least compli-cated solution would be for a lead to come from Buckingham Palace itself.

Such royal approval for a new constitutional system would be a singular service by the outgoing Queen. Of course, I doubt whether the House of Windsor has the imagination to act as an initiator of such drastic change. The idea of the Queen introducing the concept of a republic might strike some as decidedly peculiar. Yet, what other role can the Queen look forward to? The British monarchy is now the subject of ridicule and controversy, and nothing is likely to reverse this process. It is being sidelined by the new European Union. Instead of entering the history books as a monarch at bay, having constantly to react to criticism – indeed abuse – how much more edifying to use the last few years of her reign in preparing the country for what anyway is inevitable – a modern constitution? Nothing would then become her like the leaving of her office.

Should she refuse this role, then the House of Windsor will be remembered as little more than a bunch of super-rich mediocrities hanging on, against all odds, not just to their unearned privileges but to an archaic constitution which prevents their subjects from enjoying the twenty-first century.

CHRISTOPHER HITCHENS

THE PEOPLE AND THE MONARCHY

THE FRENCH PHILOSOPHER Roland Barthes made the rather
gnomic, but I think suggestive observation, that mythology in
the last instance is always located on the right. I don't think he
meant to say that there are no radical or revolutionary myths –
no Frenchman could decently say that – or revolutionary or
liberal illusions; rather that the mythic element in any ordered
society is usually there to serve some useful purpose, or at least
that it may be put to such a purpose. What I miss most in
discussion of the British monarchy is any unembarrassed
engagement with the interests served by it: not the role it plays,
or the symbolism it exerts but the interests served by monarchy
and by monarchism, not by just the Royal Family in its
contingent form.

Now I am very aware, as I hope we all are, of the complexity
and sensitivity of this topic in a very stratified society that is full
of conflicts of interest. Lord Rees-Mogg has recently shown
how easy it is, by a mere stroke of his mighty pen, to incite mass
resentment and even class warfare – and that is just within the
Tory Party.

But I think that people understand instinctively that the
monarchy serves not the Conservative Party but the conservative interest. Walter Bagehot understood this quite unhypo-
critically and was plain enough to say so in ringing prose. He
saw the Crown as an additional insurance policy against the
clamant noise of the men and women of no property. My
friend Peter Porter, the distinguished Australian poet, once
told me that it had not taken him long to work out after

landing on these shores, that the Queen was worth at the least a couple of million subliminal votes for the Tory Party and I think his poetic instinct was as sound in its way as the actuarial and utilitarian calculations of Walter Bagehot were sound in his.

The reason for the rapid decline, perhaps the extinction of the Windsor myth in Peter Porter's native Australia, and for its very deep crisis in Britain now, is precisely because elements in the establishment have come to wonder whether the Crown really does discharge its office properly as the chief magician in the realm of illusion. In other words, whether the game is worth the candle from what, in happier days, one might have got away with calling the ruling class point of view.

Now the role of the monarchy, of monarchism and the British Crown in particular, in domesticating democratic, electoral, politics and in containing and limiting that politics by a hierarchy of deference, is still hard to exaggerate. The crisis has not yet begun to touch the culture of deference.

Roy Hattersley, on one famous occasion, was offered a rather menial post as Minister of State in some rather obscure ministry and asked with the chubby eagerness for which he is renowned, in the hearing of probably one too many people, 'Does this mean I get into the Privy Council?'. He really wanted to swear an oath and he was not sure he would have arrived as a modern British politician until he had gone through a medieval oathing ceremony. The history of more than one Labour government, I submit, is inscribed in that fatuous giveaway remark, and it reminds me of my proposed one sentence Private Member's Bill, which is open to any member of any party to steal from me without acknowledgement. This bill would rename the Privy Council; it would update its antiquarian title, calling it by what it really is, The Secret Council. Think what a difference it would make if we just gave the Privy Council its right name. At one blow, it would expose the connection between the quaint medieval flummery that we all think we can see through (though we go on referring to the Privy Council as if it was as natural as breathing), and modern, bureaucratic, official secrecy in the exercise of unlawful prerogatives in Parliament.

It would also expose the tie that binds the symbol and the tradition to the brute reality and it would finally reveal the limits of really updating the system. We would not after all have advanced matters very far by bringing the Privy Council's name (the Secret Council, the Private Council) into the twentieth century and I can think of only too many highly streamlined politicians who would not mind taking it over and running it under that very name, and calling that modernisation.

We can permit ourselves to argue that the monarchy serves two functional interests. It dignifies the concealed intestinal workings of an undemocratic state and it decorates the apex of a pyramid-shaped social system. A young aspirant cadet at his military examination at Sandhurst for admission to a regimental body was asked to define the role of cavalry in modern warfare and after a pause said that it lent dash and colour to what would otherwise be an extremely vulgar brawl. There is marginal utility in that remark and it is understood by the powers that be, who have in that sense at least a very keen and developed sense of humour.

But it does something more. It provides an element of pride and consolation in the lives of those who are condemned by that politics to be mere spectators and passive consumers of the distant power game and of the battle for a larger share of this society's rewards. And my quarrel with the monarchy is precisely its success in that second area, the area in which its supporters quite rightly claim that it is most successful: its success with the unsuccessful.

Every now and then a newspaper will do a feature about some exotic islanders. I think they may be Trobrianders but it is conceivable that they may be those Gilbert and Ellice Islanders who worship Prince Philip. They display his photographs, they have little Prince Philip models, they even have propitiatory ceremonies to Prince Philip. The special symbol and rite of passage in this tribe is the wearing of a very large and elaborate penis-gourd and on one occasion when the Royal Yacht *Britannia* passed within hailing distance of the Islands, the Islanders asked if Prince Philip could perhaps be allowed to put in, that their God could come to them, don the gourd and be otherwise enshrined as the totem and juju of the tribe. It was a close run thing for the royal party on that occasion. We might laugh at them. But I don't really see how we can dare to laugh at these Trobrianders and Gilbert and Ellice Islanders.

An islander from Tuvalu or Kiribati coming to Britain, especially if he was a Polynesian anthropologist, would think, what gives here? What is the extraordinary credulity and deference of these people? What will they not believe?

My quarrel therefore, and this is the hardest thing very often to say especially for people on the left such as myself, is a quarrel with public opinion, with the psyche of the people we are always supposed to trust for their good sense and sound instinct: with the common people.

In 1988, the year in which I am proud to say I became a founder signatory of Charter 88, I made a film with Tom Nairn of his brilliant path-breaking book *The Enchanted Glass, Britain and Its Monarchy*. It was also as you will remember the anniversary of the Glorious Revolution, which Margaret Thatcher put forward as the alternative to shabby Continental experiments like the French, or subversive separatist movements like the American. We went to Brixham in Devon where William of Orange landed in 1688. The Queen was going to do a drive-by. We filmed, and then we did what you have to do for TV, we asked people what they thought about the monarchy.

One of the most depressing experiences of my life was to hear the propagandised uniformity of the responses, from people who were ordinarily cheerful, decent, democratic and rather subversive in some of their manners, who would, when asked this question, start to talk as if they were under a mild form of hypnosis. They always used the same terms. They would always say 'It's the pageantry'. 'It's the envy of the world'. 'It brings in the tourists'. There was a sort of 'doesn't it?' at the end of all these statements, which was never quite uttered, and which I decided not to take them up on. Other remarks were uniformly made. 'I wouldn't have her job'. Well, I wanted to say, no one is going to ask you. And if they did you could not say yes because you were not born in the right place, but, nonetheless, this is a very common view. 'I wouldn't do it. I wouldn't have that job'. And even the one piece of permitted criticism, that everybody knows, was always uttered in the same dull robotic tones: 'Of course I would get rid of some of those hangers on'. None of these people seemed to realise that they were *themselves* the hangers on. Until I read Ian McEwan's marvellous novel *A Child in Time*, I did not have a phrase for this reaction but McEwan found it for me when a man in some distress is reduced so much in circumstances that he spends a lot of time in despair watching day-time TV and quiz shows and chat shows, and watching what people will allow to be done to them by celebrities, subjecting themselves to public humiliations. In his memorable phrase, 'the experience of watching that is the pornography of the democrat'. It was for me as a radical, the democrat's pornography to find myself slightly despising my fellow citizens for their repetitiveness, their credulity, their deference, I would say almost their servility. These were people who had been propagandised by a hysterical, mediocre, loyalist media for decades, and by a cynical political class which well understood the utility of such vulgar bamboozlement. It was rather like a lot of England these days actually. It was like Philip Larkin without the poetry.

In that connection, I would like to take issue with Shirley Williams' view about the role played by the hereditary principle in the royalist politics of Belgium, Spain and elsewhere. Against this one can point out that the greatest movement of self-emancipation from myth as well as from power in our time, the 1989 Revolution in Russia and Eastern Europe, overthrew a system which celebrated the masses, praised and flattered the masses but denied the individual and elevated a leader-figure into a cult with divine status. The very worst of those regimes degenerated and decayed so much that they adopted the hereditary principle.

Charles Moore has on occasion celebrated the homely and healthy instinct that gives the British grocer the right to say Matthew & Son on the front of his store, as a defence of the hereditary principle. If the principle works in commerce, why not elsewhere? I offer you Ceaucescu & Son, or, as in present day North Korea, Kim Il Sung & Son, or Fidel Castro & Brother. These examples suggest that the hereditary principle is always in the service of illegitimate power and of the credulous worship of that power; an especially disgusting aspect of all propagandised systems.

I also have a quarrel to register with Baroness Williams when she says that we have had enough with press intrusion into the private lives of the Royal Family. Anyone who applauds this sentiment is a fool, a credulous fool; one must look public opinion in the face and tell it that this is what it is. You may not by definition invade your own privacy. If Princess Diana wants to go to one rag and Prince Charles to another and compete, in a bidding war with the tabloids, to vent their uninteresting private lives upon the rest of us, it is our privacy that is being invaded, and it would be I think a most excellent thing if Parliament would take some remedial step to prevent this ceaseless intrusion.

I live in the United States. It is true that there is a great generosity of spirit and breadth of mind in the United States which is proud to be a republic, founded in fact by skilful, brave, literate English gentlemen farmers who had to fight a war against a German despot and German Hessian mercenaries for their freedom. It was a war in which England and the best kind of English tradition won and German despotism lost and it is only a pity that these gentlemen farmers did not finish the job with George III. The United States Constitution and the documents composed by the founding fathers show it. If you want to instill your children with pride in a great English tradition, get them to read the founding documents of the American Constitution, and get John Patten to pay for it if you can.

Who does not know, as right-wingers like to point out, that the Soviet Union used to have a constitution of some merit and that it did not do them any good at all? Now, if you don't *have* freedom there is no point in writing down that you do have it; that is true. But I know a far better example. There is one country in the world that has virtually duplicated the United States Constitution including, word for word, all the basic rights of the 23 amendments. That country is Liberia. So it is as evident, as it should be to anybody, that the mere inscription of a constitution does not guarantee liberty. Anyone who lives in Washington can tell you that. Most of the great political battles in the United States are to safeguard the Constitution from its American foes, from those who would try to short-circuit it, from those who refuse to act in its principles. That is what politics is about in the United States and that is as it should be. The combat ought to be unending, carried on to humane and democratic and above all *intelligible* standards.

The supporters of monarchy insist that the Crown gives us respect, and that it is imbued with tradition – that this monarchial element is splendid and magnificent. I think we can requite the two demands of our monarchists. One, by being *self* governing and *self*-respecting. And the second by not letting the element of history and tradition depart from us. The best traditions of English tolerance and freedom can be embodied in a modern form. I think if we set out on this road we would shortly find not just that we had left monarchy behind but that we did not miss it.

MARTIN AMIS

MY IMAGINATION AND I

THE ONLY IMAGINATION we know anything for sure about is our own. And I have to report that I am utterly unexercised by the Royal Family. I don't care, one way or the other. Of course I helplessly house all the usual junk in my head. I recently had a sex dream, for instance, about the Duchess of York: you may be touched – and surprised to learn that I found Fergie to be both a considerate and an inventive lover. But my waking mind doesn't care about any of them.

This book may turn out to be the most significant royal achievement of the modern era. However anachronistic, marginal and degraded, the monarchy, somehow can still excite eloquent debate. But not from me. Because I don't care. (Why *do* people care, quite so much? I reluctantly assume that there is a kind of counter-snobbery at work – as passionate, and as susceptible to charisma, as its opposite.) The moralist could argue, surely unassailably, that the Royal Family has no business being what and where it is. The actuary could claim that in fact they pay their way (tourism? exports? magazine sales?) Students and guardians of the constitution, including the fieriest republicans, would have to be daunted by the prospect of abolition: throttling the flower of the leisure class looks like a leisure-class undertaking in itself. Too much time and trouble. It isn't worth it.

Americans, we are often told, prefer their soap operas to be about rich people; we prefer our soap operas to be about poor people. Nevertheless, the soap opera that we live with, and finance, is about rich people: the Rise and Fall of the House of

Windsor. This soap is clearly falling apart; it is repetitive, formulaic and queasy with insincerity; it whines to be put out of its misery. Let me adduce the parallel of the literary protagonist. Literature used to be about gods; then demi-gods; then kings, soldiers, fabulous lovers; then the upper classes; then the middle classes; then you and me; and then *them* (those below). The Royal Family has completed this declension in the space of a single generation. The Queen may be a self-pitying miser, but until very recently she was still hedged with the vestiges of divinity. Her children have had their moments as soldiers and lovers – Andrew wedged into a helicopter, Charles kissing his bride on the balcony, to vast applause – but they are well on their way to being you and me, or even *them*: figures of pity and ridicule, hopelessly compromised, hopelessly exposed.

Like everyone else, the royals, in other words – in Yeats's words:

> have fallen in the dreams the ever living
> breathe on the tarnished mirror of the world,
> and then smooth out with ivory hands and sigh.

There is no need to dismantle the monarchy. It might have made us feel more grown-up to do the job ourselves, but as it turns out contemporary forces are doing it for us. This process is happening not only to an institution but also to a group of individuals. So I suggest we sit back and – with some sympathy, without too much relish – observe the spectacle.

SIR JOHN STOKES

KEEP THE QUEEN

I FIND IT very difficult to put into words one's deepest feelings and beliefs which I have about the monarchy, as I have about the Church, as I have about the history of England. Do we need a head of state? Of course we do. And we need a monarchy, and foreigners would think us mad if we questioned the role of the monarchy, which is admired so much throughout the world as well as in this country. Indeed, our monarchy is the envy of many other nations.

The monarch embodies the whole nation and gives us a sense of history, continuity and cohesion, which I believe no other institution does. A president is often a retired politician, for instance M. Mitterand, and I believe would be a very poor substitute for the Queen. And the Queen receives respect and deference in a way that no ordinary politician would do. We remember the Queen was anointed and crowned at her coronation and therefore is a quasi-religious person.

She is also someone to whom all oaths are made, all oaths of loyalty. Not to the minister of defence, in the case of a soldier, but to the Queen in person. That I believe is very important. She is a focus of loyalty which no other person could provide. The government can send you to war, to be killed. It is very important if you are going to war, your oath is to the Queen, and not to the whomever it may be, the secretary of state for defence. Very important. And I believe in this country of ours, where the manners and morals are going down day-by-day and have been for some time, we still see the highest standards of chivalry, honour, integrity in the armed forces, which are certainly the best in the world and the best people in the country.

We have heard much about the so-called 'old-fashioned' ceremonies of the coronation and of the opening of Parliament, but I believe most ordinary people think these are splendid occasions, which cheer the whole nation and cannot be copied in any other way. Tradition, symbolism, splendour, pageantry, reminds us of our past and encourages us, I believe, for the future, to be true to that great past. It reminds us also of the continuity of our history as an island race, unconquered for over 900 years, as I frequently remind my French friends. It tells us the sort of people we really are and gives us a pride in our past which few other nations can equal.

The monarchy here survived for a thousand years, and apart from the papacy is the oldest institution in Europe. We love monarchy so much that when we did have a republic from 1649 to 1660, those eleven years, we called the King back without a shot being fired or a blow being offered. A very remarkable occasion. Intellectuals and constitutional theorists have very little idea how popular the throne is with ordinary people. I think now of my constituents, the man in the shop, the man in the pub, the woman at her meeting in the afternoon, whatever it may be, or those in factories. The monarchy is extremely popular with the non-intellectual part of the population who have the deepest patriotism. And those who would replace monarchy by a presidential form of government have little contact, I believe, with the feelings of ordinary people.

It would be a dreadful mistake now, because of the media coverage, because of the misbehaviour of at least two members of the Royal Family, that we should decide to abolish the monarchy and remove the Queen. I was reading my hero Wellington's letters the other day, and just before Waterloo he wrote to a friend, 'What dreadful times we all live in. The King is mad and the Regent is a horrible man.' We went on to win the battle of Waterloo.

I believe the monarchy is the most precious part of our constitution, which of course is composed of the Queen, Lords and Commons. And I say this now, only recently having left the Commons, at a time when members of that House are not perhaps as much respected as they used to be. We must be thankful that we still have an hereditary monarch and dare I say it, hereditary peers in the House of Lords, who are not in it for publicity, or for gain, or for career, or to be a cabinet minister. Furthermore they have done something in life, whereas some of the people in the House of Commons have done nothing except be party politicians. And I believe that democracy needs to have some curbs. I don't believe it is a complete answer to every problem. I think the hereditary system, handing down from father to son, is very important. A reassuring link with our past. And I believe it also produces, very often, a rather superior person to those who are elected.

Therefore, I believe we should have pride and thankfulness for our history, and above all for our monarch, and show gratitude to her for 40 years of unstinted service and devotion to the nation at a time when public service is not as good as it might be. A president could not do nearly as much, nearly so well.

SUE TOWNSEND

Do You Believe in Fairies?

I AM FROM the working class and, just because you are successful in any one field, it doesn't mean that you cease to be working-class. My accent is ironed out a bit, I've got an Aga now, but you can't take the working class out of the girl, not completely.

Recently I've been working on a council estate and I have to tell you that the conditions there are now so bad that children have forgotten how to play. The men have vanished and are living in Wales for some reason, after impregnating the women. They have no work and they have no reason to get out of bed in the morning. It is a dangerous state of affairs and it is a result of our terrible class system, which strangles people, wastes their lives and wastes their talents. I have to say that I see the Royal Family at the apex of this class system.

I have absolutely nothing against the present Royal Family as people. I don't know them. God knows, they've proved their fallibility over the last few years and there are more revelations to come. They probably won't shock people any more, we're hardened to it, but when I was a child the Queen's portrait looked down on me as I sat in my classroom struggling to learn my nine times table. The Queen's portrait was in every classroom of that school; she was an icon. I believed in her. I believed in fairies too. And I believed in Santa Claus. I believed in God and I believed in Jesus. One by one, I've stopped believing in them all.

I stopped believing in fairies first. I stopped believing in God when our alcoholic headmistress kept the school in and spoke for an hour and a half, while girls fainted around her, about the Christian sin of not wearing the school beret. The Royal Family and God went together. In fact at that time we were still being taught that the Royal Family had been ordained by God, that they were the representatives of God on earth, and I really believed that the Royal Family could cure leprosy.

So I stopped believing in the Royal Family at an early age. Of course, being an English person then, you couldn't talk about sex, and you couldn't talk about death. By debating the monarchy, we're breaking the last taboo, and it's time we did. I'm sick of this British timidity about institutions, they're all in a mess. It's time that we looked critically at them all, including the monarchy. I really am very frightened about the hereditary principle as well – we came very near to having the Duke of Windsor as king but luckily he fell for the sexual allure of Mrs Simpson. He was notorious for the opinion that Hitler did have a point of view. So I do worry about William being hit on the head by that golf-club. Has the boy been examined carefully or will he too have to be siphoned away at some point in the future?

Those who defend the monarchy talk about the glorious pageantry that we have, the fun and the ceremonial that we do so well. I say that we could keep these, we don't have to do away with them, we can keep as many uniforms as we like and we can even invent new ceremonies. So let's do it! The thing that keeps this country together is big football matches, Frank Bruno, and the Eurovision Song Contest. We need better quality songs and rituals. We have some of the best people in the world, the best musicians, the best actors, the best writers and theatre directors, so why haven't we got them?

Finally, I would like to deal with republicanism. Barcelona is one of my favourite cities in the whole world. It's a beautiful city architecturally, and it's a republican stronghold. The citizens are feisty people who stroll around; the King is not welcome there. It's perfectly possible to live in a republic and to be happy, to be challenged, to be brave and not to kow-tow to people. They are human beings just as we are. We need to build some Barcelonas in Britain. The law would be king, the law would be queen. Then people would be happier – we would be more ourselves, not less.

FAY WELDON

ON HAVING A QUEEN AND A STATE RELIGION BOTH

BRITAIN HAS A state religion with the monarch at its head. This is not an inevitable state of affairs. But it is quite cosy. It means we imbue our institutions with a certain romance and dignity, from Inland Revenue (we pay our taxes to the Queen) to the Post Office (the words Royal Mail make it feel somewhat treasonable for anyone to rob a mail train; years later we find ourselves still talking about that Great Train Robbery). And when we write C of E – Church of England – on a form, that being the conventional thing to do, and easier than explaining the particular area of secular thought we happen to inhabit, we are making a statement of subjecthood. It doesn't do any harm, we say, and it even feels quite nice, as if we were somehow part of something – and we know that to the hospital or the school or whoever's form it is we're filling in, it means that we don't expect to eat strange foods, take unusual religious holidays, or suddenly take our shoes off in strange places. It means we will for the most part behave like the generality of those around us; British people, members of the Church of England.

Well, at least that's how it used to be. These days vegetarians can turn out to be C of E, women turn out to be priests, the night mail is all but done away with, the Queen's own secret intelligence service spies on her, and she's even expected to pay tax to herself. How far distant is the day when it was all her money, at least in name, and you could persuade people to pay it to the monarch even if you couldn't get them to hand it over to the sheriff or the temporal power. God had put the king in his place and it suited the sheriff to have him there; oh, very well!

The other day I heard a little old lady say 'Oh the Royals have different blood than ours, completely different, it's hereditary, you know.' Just because that is untrue, it does not mean that it is not a source of comfort and contentment to the powerless. Who are we in our loud clever brash way to take these comforts away from people who need them?

But just as the vote is no longer sufficient in itself to protect the interests of the working man in which I include woman, of course – neither is the existence of the monarchy sufficient to keep the undereducated, underhoused, underemployed and our increasingly alienated young either comforted or contented. There has to be change, and I fear the quickest and cheapest and easiest and most revolutionary way of bringing about change is to do away with the monarchy. I say 'afraid' because, believe me, that is what I do feel. Afraid.

'Children hold on tight to Nurse', I find myself saying, as Hillaire Belloc said at the turn of the century. 'Children hold on tight to Nurse, for fear of finding something worse.' Mrs Thatcher, say, as president in Buckingham Palace? I ask you, who else would people want as queen under another title?

What I think we English want at the moment – forgive me, Scotland, Ireland, Wales; this royal stuff is traditionally English – is a new Royal Family. We're in the habit of having them. We got tired of the Stuarts; so tired we beheaded Charles. Having got so much more tired of not having a monarch, whimsical to the last, we brought back his son. We found Charles II too frivolous, so we brought in the boring Hanoverians; and then all those brothers went mad – obviously the hereditary principle could go very wrong. So how about little Victoria? Miles from the true succession but never mind; if we don't mention it no one will notice – and they were quite right, the female line didn't go mad and proved wonderfully enduring. It took just a smartish switch of name to Windsor during world wars to lose the German connection. But now Victoria's line is tired and dusty – we think it's time for a change, new faces, new genes, fresh new style. This lot simply don't *look* royal enough. We look at our Royals too closely in the press and on TV; we see very little in their faces of the Divine Right of Kings. Perhaps we know too much about genetics to accept the hereditary principle any more? Perhaps we'd better try electing them and not trust any more to God's divine providence. Then at least we can fire them, vote them out, if all doesn't go well.

But how boring: how sensible. What, are we to have no element of chance? We put up with it when conceiving our children, after all. I am not a true anti-monarchist. What does our monarchy cost us a year? One Trident missile? You can't gossip about a Trident missile as you can about Fergie. But I am swayed by one thing. And that is the fate of our children: granted, conceived by the hereditary principle, product of pure chance themselves. I want the nation's children to have a moral and intelligent education. I don't want them to be taught superstition and old desert faiths, or new psychotic ones either. A moral education and a religious education are not the same thing. Values may be eternal but we can't behave as if they were; who these days acts as if they were? I don't want to have Christian schools, Muslim schools, Jewish schools, Catholic schools; I do not want our children educated into the cruel and superstitious faiths of our limited and ancient forefathers. I do not want my perfectly moral and thoughtful children made to sit at school under the 'cross', this image of a tortured half-God, half-Man. Children aren't even expected to put up with Noddy; how can they put up with this lamentable symbol? It can do them no good. In order to preserve their equanimity they are as likely to identify with the crucifiers as the crucified, and act accordingly.

Nor do I want to see my neighbours' children learning about my God in order to reject Him. There are altogether too many Gods about. Nor is it pleasant for the children of families who worship minority Gods to feel excluded from the wider community outside the school. If parents insist on indoctrinating their children, let them do it in the privacy of their own homes, and if they feel that the only way to teach children to love their neighbour, and how to be good not bad, and bear some kind of responsibility for others, for society at large, is through Christianity or Islam or Judaism or Moonie-ism or Scientology, I suppose they better had – if your belief is that any religion is better than none. But it seems pretty pathetic to me, to treat religion as a means of socialising the young; as a tool for their conditioning.

In the last Education Act, in 1993, as it was sighing its last breath through the House of Lords, an amendment was snuck in at the dead of night: that there was to be a Christian act of worship in our schools every day. And the result was that, unobserved, all our state schools became in effect church schools overnight and I do not like to see that. The Muslims, as things stand, have a perfect right to ask to have their own religious schools. The Christians have them; why not us, they ask? Why not? I could give you a hundred reasons, from the *fatwah* downwards, from the subjection of women to the ghettoisation of our immigrant communities, but there is, as things stand, no justification for forbidding any group the right to bring up its children in the schools of its faith, to indoctrinate them in whatever unpleasant absurdity they wish, from the Moonies to the Christians to the acts and attitudes of the British upper classes – and if it takes the disestablishment of the Church, via the abolition of the monarchy, to achieve the final division of Church from State and intellectual and spiritual freedom for our children then that's it. Goodbye, monarchy.

'Children, drop the hand of Nurse,
and hope to God it won't get worse.'

We can have a state religion without a monarchy at its head. We can re-read the mind of God and appoint ourselves a female English Pope. We can be a secular state. We can have a monarchy and not a state religion. We can do anything we like.

But a country with both a state religion and a monarchy at its head is just going to bumble its way into confusion and hypocrisy. Each institution brings the other into disrepute. Something has got to give and I suspect it's going to have to be the monarchy.

JONATHAN CLARK

THE PERILS OF DISESTABLISHMENT

IF I WERE to offer one piece of advice to Charter 88, it is that they should seize on a central issue – the disestablishment of the Church of England – if they want to secure many other items on their agenda. By the same token, anyone who wants to resist the rest of Charter 88's agenda ought to defend the current status of the Church of England.

History helps us to understand these phenomena by setting them in a wider framework. Let me briefly give you three examples of history upstaging current polemic. Marina Warner suggests that monarchy had long been defended by taboo, but that now people no longer refrain from taking part in imagining the society we want. That's a ringing phrase, but it shouldn't convince historians because historians know that people have done just that for centuries – imagining the society that they want. While some of those people have indeed been republican, most have been royalist. Far from being cocooned by taboo, the monarchy has always been at the centre of constitutional controversy. If controversy has been slightly muted since 1945, it has only been on the good principle, 'if it is not broken do not mend it'. English society has always been exceptionally vocal and participatory by comparison with many equivalent states. Historically this is not inconsistent with monarchy.

Secondly, Marina Warner also suggests that the moment has now come (a ringing but historically meaningless phrase) to examine the monarchy and to describe its function in terms of notions like fiction and disguise and symbol; inverted commas hang in the air around these terms. A historian again might reply that not only is there nothing special about the present moment, but that if we are to use these terms we must use them of all arguments equally, including the arguments of Charter 88. They may indeed be strong arguments, but we have to ask in what sense is a Bill of Rights symbolic; what fictions does proportional representation rest on? In his subtle study *Inventing the People* Edmund Morgan has shown how the fictions of absolute monarchy passed into the fictions of universal democracy, which is an even more dramatic example of this point.

My third premise is that history reveals that even our favourite descriptions of monarchy are part of the debate. They are moves in the game, not authoritative and impartial pronouncements. Walter Bagehot is often looked up to as an authority. He was a journalist of the 1860s. He wrote his famous book *The English Constitution* in 1867 and he encouraged his contemporaries – or at least the intelligentsia among his contemporaries – to think that the rationalising, steam intellect England of Queen Victoria had in fact already become essentially republican but with an anomalous and an ineffective figurehead sovereign perched on top who was defended only by taboo, myth and ritual. He says virtually nothing about the Church of England. He says virtually nothing about the value of religion to society. His thesis is that there is a theatre of the monarchy and when the population grow up, when they become rational and educated, it would no longer be necessary. Was that right?

There are two corrections to be made here. In the first place, when the letters of Queen Victoria came to be published in the early twentieth century, it was shown that she had real power and used it – not just those three rights, to be consulted, to encourage and to warn, that Bagehot had credited her with. Secondly, in the very year that Bagehot published *The English Constitution*, the Second Reform Act was passed, beginning that enormous widening of the franchise which eventually proved that society at large was much less republican than he thought it was.

I will now bring this to a focus on the question of

disestablishment. Let me suggest at the outset that there is no such thing as modernity. That is to say, all ages are equally modern to themselves. There is no sense in which secularisation or disestablishment are dictated to us by history with a capital H. So it follows (my second point) that if there is an erosion of myths of royalty in the very recent past, this is not evidence of a process of growing up nationally. It is not just part of a natural process of discarding myth for a rational mature politics. It is just a reflection of attacks on the Royals. Those attacks require specific explanations and not general explanations. Third, there have always been really rather few serious republicans in England. There have indeed been some, some have been quite important, but ultimately rather few mattered. We need particular explanations of why it is that those few cases have actually arisen at all. I argue that those few were often men and women who had a theological objection to the monarchy and especially to a monarch as head of the Church.

Fourth, this is still true. It is still important because effective change usually comes from *within* great institutions and not because of pressure or assaults from without. Reform normally comes from within, and that is still the case with the Church of England. The clergy who are most reported in the press as being eager to use the recent difficulties of the Royal Family to press for disestablishment are those evangelicals and liberals who reject the thesis that the Church of England is the Church of all the English because it is the lineal descendant of the medieval Catholic Church in this realm. Fifth, I conclude, therefore, that the most likely route to disestablishment will not be from whatever Charter 88 does, but from the Church of England's internal debates, especially that on women priests. In the seventeenth century, the equation 'no bishop, no king' proved to be true when the Presbyterian attack on episcopacy led to the fall of the monarchy. Today, the formula is 'no priest, no bishop, no king'. Assert the validity of women's ordination and eventually episcopacy is undermined; this can only have a knock-on effect on the monarchy.

The Archbishop of Canterbury opposes disestablishment

for reasons that Charles Moore might approve. But he apparently fails to understand the historical logic which his support for women's ordination entails. There is one other minor possibility, that a strengthened European Parliament would try to legislate to break the tie between Church and State in England in the name of the harmonisation of constitutional practice in a secular, rational European Community. Something similar happened in America: when the United States were set up in 1787, the Federal Government deliberately took those powers. That I think is less likely. The immediate prospect is the impact of women priests.

For these reasons I take the view that the consequences of disestablishment will be very extensive, and felt in many walks of life. The Church could no longer credibly anoint an incoming monarch. The claim that the government was a sacred trust and the claim that the nation was an object of divine providence would be implicitly surrendered. National affairs would be profoundly secularised. That would be, I think, a step towards secularisation rather than a gain in religious liberty. And it is notable in the recent debate on the monarchy and disestablishment that it is not the sects of Protestant dissent or the Roman Catholic Church that are calling for the disestablishment of the Church of England. It is certain Anglican clergymen themselves.

Following disestablishment, the monarchy would be appraised in merely secular and functional terms. If the monarchy were forced to operate in that setting, it would eventually succumb in the snake pit of secular politics. A secular, an elected, and a presidential head of state would come as part of a package with sweeping constitutional reform including proportional representation. That in turn would damage a parliament which could no longer claim to be integral with the monarchy in the historical institutions of government. Parliament would thereby be diminished in its own claims to legitimacy.

These are all in a sense backward-looking historical observations. I will finally take off my historian's mortarboard and offer you a personal and forward-looking reaction.

We are always faced with a problem in national politics: how do we embody our highest ideals in national institutions? There has always been a debate within political thought between theories which say that authority ascends from below and theories which say that authority descends from above. We still have to try to reconcile those two ideas of authority in our national life. Pure unalloyed democracy asserts that authority ascends from below; deference to our ideals alone implies that it descends from above and that we are dictated to by those ideals. Clearly we want to be both democratic and moral; but this is not as easy as we are led to believe. Look at what happens in different polities when they try to deal with practical problems which produce a schism in these respects.

Take abortion. In the United States, a society with a high level of religious belief and observance but a resolutely and militantly secularised central government, the debate is polarised between two militant extremes; one asserting the woman's right to choose, the other asserting the right of the unborn child. These can hardly be reconciled in a secular framework. In England, somehow, in a society in which we still manage to embody our sense of ideals and our sense of democratic accountability in a polity which is humanised, and which is dignified by an established Church and therefore an established morality, we seem to have found a compromise which indeed satisfies none of the extremists on either side but which is a fairer account of how to take an agonising decision like this in a complex world.

The breakdown of establishment would promote the breakdown of moral consensus. I am keenly conscious of the English state as an experiment in government which was set up in the 1530s with the break from Rome. It may have had its trajectory. It may be that the state, essentially formulated then, greatly modified, greatly challenged as it has been in the centuries since, is now meeting challenges which imply its essential dissolution. I fear its dissolution now will be an extremely unhappy process. I fear that we are facing a prospect of our national life unravelling. We would abandon our past without acquiring a vision of the future. If that happens then the second half of my adult life will be an unhappy one.

JAMES FENTON

WHO ARE THEY TO JUDGE THE PRINCE?

I TAKE IT that the Archdeacon of York is a member of the Princess of Wales's party and that his supporters among the general public are the Princess's supporters. I take it like this because I cannot otherwise see why the archdeacon should start worrying now whether the Prince of Wales should succeed to the throne.

It is not a pressing issue, is it? No, it is not pressing. The issue arises only if what you are trying to say is: the previous week's speech by the Princess shows that she has been badly treated. It was Diana's tears that moved Mr Austin.

If we were talking common sense about a common matter, experience would tell us that it is absolutely unwise to pass judgement on the break-up of a marriage, even a break-up we have observed closely. But the Archdeacon of York is not dealing in common sense. His views are absurd. He should get a grip on himself.

Then comes the unctuous follow-up from assorted Anglicans who say that the Prince should go back to Diana, confess his sins, repent before Diana and God, and patch up his marriage. And somewhere thrown in you will find a mild sentence to the effect that she, Diana, might have a bit of repenting to do as well. But no one of Diana's party likes to emphasise that side of things. That is not what the faction is for.

'Go back' is easily said when it is not you who has to do the going back. Even easier is to say it when there does not seem to be the foggiest chance that your advice will be taken up. Easiest

97

of all is to say 'Go back' when there has not been the least public hint that the Prince would be welcome if he did come back, even after whatever act of repentance these unctuous Anglicans envisage has been performed.

Let's say the Prince does not go back. That leaves the Princess's faction within the Church of England divided along the following lines. One lot says that this adulterous prince should not be king. The other lot says (perhaps after having had the constitutional position patiently explained to them) that, OK, we cannot oppose his being king on these grounds, but we can at least stop him being head of the Church. If necessary, we will disestablish the Church, in order to stop this scandalous man becoming its head.

My view on this is that there are scandals and scandals. The Prince's private life may be scandalous in the etymological sense that it has given rise to a great deal of clucking of tongues. But the establishment of the Church of England is a scandal of quite different proportions, and no less a scandal because the tongues have long since ceased to cluck.

For a church that pretends to look to the teaching of the Gospels, and that contrives to become an arm of the legislature, seems to me a scandal. A church that submits nominations of its bishops to the temporal powers seems highly scandalous.

A church that eagerly involves itself in court intrigue (which is what we are seeing) in order to promote the advantage of a fallen princess, to recommend that the succession be changed in order to thwart the heir to the throne, is a church that really ought to be called to order, both by its own congregation and by the secular powers.

One could say of the Prince that, however embarrassing some of the results, there is a congruence between his efforts to be a prince and our notion of what a prince might be. He cultivates sporting and artistic skills. He is trained in the art of war. He has laid out a garden and been praised for it. He feels concern over a range of public issues, not least over that great issue: what a prince might do, what role he might play, in the unfolding of our public life. And I think even the love of a certain number of women fits easily into our idea of what a prince might get up to, without forfeiting our respect for him *qua* prince. Now look at the Church of England and see how it compares with the mission set forth in the Gospels and by the early church. Do Anglicans eagerly seek and embrace opportunities for martyrdom? They are martyrs to chilblains, perhaps, but that is as far as it goes. Do they have, like the Son of Man, no place to lay their heads? No, they are like foxes and the birds of the air – they have their nests and holes, and they build palaces for their bishops. Are they persecuted for Christ? No, the Church has much preferred a persecuting role. Today Anglicans persecute Prince Charles in Christ's name.

Do they, as Christ did, cast out devils? Er, no. Do they heal the sick by miraculous means? No, they frown on that side of the business. Do they preach that the time is fast approaching when all things shall be fulfilled? Well, not to the extent of going out with the sandwich boards, and not on 'Thought for the Day'.

No, the Church does not conform to any reasonable idea of what Christ's mission might be. Indeed, it seems in many respects quite the opposite of such a mission. So the real question is: if we have a prince who, in most respects, represents a version of what we expect a prince to be, and a church which historically craves the protection of the monarch as its head, plus an entree into the legislature and other perks, is it not unfair to ask of this prince-who-is-like-a-prince that he should become head of this church-which-is-not-like-a-church? This scandalous church. This adulterated assembly.

The Church is supposed to be the bride of Christ, not the court accomplice of Diana. If it is prevailed upon by the Princess's faction, it should not be allowed, on spurious grounds, to reject the Prince as its head. The Church should be disestablished, but it should be done fairly and squarely.

From the secular side it should be admitted that the bishops have absolutely no business in the House of Lords, and the Prime Minister has no proper interest in appointing bishops. From the Church's side, let them become a church and not some camp game. If they want disestablishment, they should admit the Prince has nothing whatever to do with anything in this argument.

It has been said that 38 percent of Synod looks forward to disestablishment – a minority, but substantial. No doubt there is another percentage which looks forward to a kind of disestablishment through the back door, by blaming the heir to the throne, about whose life they know only the gossip. I think the whole lot of them should be disestablished whether they like it or not.

CLAIRE RAYNER

KNIT YOUR OWN ROYALS

WHEN I JOINED *Woman's Own* magazine in 1966, after seven years of assorted freelancing for medical journals, teenage magazines and the like, I was told that there were three cardinal rules for success.

One, *always* look for WTs – womb tremblers – the stories that make women shudder with fellow feeling.

Two, *never* write about anything nasty – like sex, birth and death – except with impenetrable euphemisms.

Three, *whenever possible* get a royal into the story, as *Women's Own* was the original Knit Your Own Royal Family magazine. At that point it owed its pride of place in the women's weekly market place to the fact that it had serialised, in the 1950s, the memoirs of Crawfie, governess to the little princesses in the 30s and 40s. Ever since then, I was told, the Royals had been money in the bank for the magazine and all its imitators.

I managed to survive on the magazine for twenty-two years in spite of breaking the first two rules – especially the second – pretty successfully. But I never managed to dodge the third. Even though I was writing medical and social stories and had nothing to do with royal features, there were lots of times when I too was sucked into the royal mill. When Princess Anne developed ovarian cysts, I had to explain them to the readers and speculate on her future ability to be a mother (I got it right – what a relief!) When Princess Margaret had a lung removed, there I was again – although this time I was able to point out that she was a smoker. When Diana gave birth to her babies, I had to write an enormous amount of stuff on the problems of young mothers. This wasn't easy as the letters I got from the young mothers among our readers rarely came from those living in vast palaces cushioned by large domestic staffs.

There was never any question in my mind about which of the features in the magazine were regarded as the most important. We had our own specialist royal correspondent. The magazine took huge pride in its special relationship with the Palace – the press office, that is – and any journalist who didn't share the general monarchism learned to keep her mouth shut and any signs of nascent republicanism well under wraps.

It was not only *Woman's Own* that operated like this. So did all the other women's magazines; if one found out that another had a royal cover or a major royal story, the anguish and breast-beating was considerable. Attempts to produce spoilers were far from unknown. It's not surprising. It was estimated that putting Princess Diana's photograph on the cover added at least 20,000 sales to the weekly issue, probably more. The magazine's appetite for pomp and Palace gossip seemed impossible to sate.

That royal hunger lasted for a long time, but over the last decade it has changed. In the early days the tone had always been reverent and the adjectives 'radiant' and 'gracious' were heavily used. As the years went on, the tone became a little less respectful. There wasn't exactly criticism, but there was a new touch of levity. For example, sometime in 1985 I was pushed yet again into writing a piece about the Princess of Wales. I can't remember the peg I had to use, but somewhere in the article I amused myself with a term which I fully expected the subs to cut. I referred to the 'Di-olatory' that seemed to have overtaken the nation when it contemplated the Princess of Wales. To my amazement the word was left in! I braced myself for abuse from readers. I was sure they would be mortally offended by my rudeness. I received not a single letter of complaint. Similarly, when *Chat*, a down-market publication, was launched in October 1985, its cover offer was a *real* knit your own Royal Family – an offer of free patterns for royal dolls. It was such a great hit with the readers (handmade toys and dolls always are, as a matter of fact), that in June 1987 they followed up with another cover story – knit your own general election, with instructions for making Maggie Thatcher, Neil Kinnock, David Steel and David Owen. Who says women's magazines can't be witty? Interestingly, the instructions were exactly the same for each of the three men, while Maggie's design was all her own. A fair reflection of the politics of the time, perhaps.

Meanwhile, the newspapers were going at the Royal Family full tilt. It was a rare issue of a tabloid that didn't carry a royal item, and sometimes they were massive in length. I was also working for the *Sunday Mirror* – I was a busy freelance – by the time Prince Charles and Lady Diana Spencer became engaged. The major scoop of the engagement period was the story about the royal train. Did or did not this pair – as yet unblessed by archbishop or TV wedding coverage – spend a night together on the royal train while it sat in a railway siding? Palace denials were flying about like leaves in Vallambrosa. The fuss was huge. So, as I recall, were the increased sales.

Later still, on the *Sunday Mirror*, I recall a singularly odd feature. A comic strip purported to show the home life of our own dear Waleses. The young mother was running after her naughty little boy, father was doing – well, not much at all really – and Mother-in-Law was popping in and out (Grandma too, sometimes). It was supposed to show that the Royals lived a cosily domestic life. Just like us, really. This strip died after a few months. I suspect this was not because of its content but because it was drawn so villainously.

At the *Sunday Mirror* I was also expected to make an occasional comment on royal issues at the top of my problem page. I tried to resist, but usually gave in to *force majeure* – the editor, that is. One thing I am sure about: I never received a letter from any reader seeking help with personal problems in which they compared themselves to the Royals. Sometimes people said they were 'like the girl in the song' or even, on occasion, that they were like a character in a current soap opera. Never was there any identification of the sort that that comic strip supposed was possible.

So even then, the readers of popular magazines and newspapers were less enamoured of the Royals than journalists thought. It began to appear that the passion for royal stories was more journalist-led than reader-led. Since the magazines I worked with had always insisted that they acted not as trend setters but as mirrors, reflecting what their readers wanted, there was an obvious gap between them and their customers.

How are matters now? Is that gap still there? Or have the readers become further addicted to royal material? Do they still buy masses of papers and magazines in order to get their fix?

I've been making a few spot checks to find out. I asked *Chat* whether they expected to find readers as interested in royals as they used to be. I was told that they do not. 'They're sated – the deference has gone,' I was told. 'We think twice now about a royal feature. We'd still do one but it would be irreverent now. There's no awe, and there is criticism.' As for the cover: 'We research our magazine with panels of readers, and they're very aware. One group told us 'If we see a royal on the cover of a magazine now, we think they must be "doing badly" '.

Similarly, the editor of *Hello* told me that the last time she used a Princess Diana cover it had no effect on sales at all. In the old days it would have added a sizeable group of readers. This time sales were healthy, but there was no marked leap in the figures.

TV coverage of the Royals has also changed. On *Good Morning with Anne and Nick* on BBC1 issues of the day are lifted from the newspapers, and viewers are invited to call in with comments and opinions. Lately, many of these topics have been royal stories, and more and more callers say they don't want any more coverage of the Royals. *Please*. Some of them say it is because they want the Royals left in peace. They're staunchly royalist and want them to be less badgered. But a sizeable number say they're thoroughly bored by it all. As one caller put it, 'You lot are trying to feed us like geese, and we want no more of it'.

It's clear to me that the public is ahead of journalists in its attitude to royal coverage. Unless there is the promise of something salacious and outrageous, in which case the public is still as avid as it would be for similar stories about soap or film stars, people really don't care very much. It's the journalists who do – and this is a sinister fact as the journalistic passion for anything royal means that important issues may fail to get the coverage they need and deserve. I can give you a concrete example.

In December 1992 Southwark Council launched a campaign intended to reduce the incidence of domestic violence and get help to women faster. It was a very unusual initiative, involving not just the council but the Metropolitan Police and a wide range of voluntary and statutory bodies in the field working together. It is a model that could be applied nationally. Not the most glamorous story perhaps, but an undoubted womb-trembler for the many, many women who are the victims of domestic violence and of great importance to the people who pick up the bills for its painful effects. The council set up a press conference, and on the morning of December 9th did a ring-round of local, regional and national media. By 12 noon, Thames TV, BBC Newsroom South-East, GLR, LBC and the *Evening Standard* had booked to attend. the *Guardian* and the *Independent* were interested, though they didn't commit themselves.

What happened? In the words of Zena Fernandes, the Southwark Council press officer:

'Just one hour later the press coverage we had worked so hard to get fell apart. One by one, media agencies cancelled as news quickly emerged that John Major would be making a statement in the Commons on the Prince and Princess of Wales's marriage.

'By the end of the day no-one was even remotely interested in covering the conference.

'On the morning of Thursday 11 December, an attempt was made to resuscitate press interest in the domestic violence campaign. When questioned as to why the launch was still not going to be covered, one radio station, GLR, said that the domestic violence launch "would sit oddly with the royal story" '.

I have to admit an interest here; I had been asked to help with the launch and had agreed to speak to the various radio and TV stations. It was an impressive effort by Southwark and it seemed to me that it could indeed save lives. It would certainly prevent a lot of misery. Yet not one single section of the media reported it.

The media had to cover the royal separation. No-one would argue with that. Even the *Independent,* which had launched itself with the solemn promise never to cover any royal matters, crumpled under the onslaught. It was there with the rest of the pack, reporting every breathless moment from the House of Commons. But surely they didn't have to exclude the domestic violence story altogether? GLR's phrase said it all. Stories about real life domestic violence and discussions about how to prevent it would 'sit oddly with the royal story'.

It was this episode, and one or two others of the same sort, that influenced my own way of working thereafter. Because of my association with people's problems, I'm often asked to take part in conferences and events of various kinds. Over the years, I've rarely refused to do so, unless a clash of dates makes it impossible. This has been a busy part of my working life for thirty years.

Now I refuse to attend any event that is open to the press and which will be attended by a royal, and most particularly by the Princess of Wales. I see no point in it. The journalists and photographers turn out all right, but not in order to give any sensible coverage to the event. They are there only to record what the royal person is wearing, what the royal did or did not say and how kind and gracious the said royal was or wasn't. The real issues become lost at best, distorted at worst. A recent example involves the Princess of Wales at a conference on eating illnesses. This young woman, who is one of the most famous victims of an eating disorder and who always looks stunning (as indeed she should with all the help that a limitless purse can provide) stood up and said, in effect, 'Don't starve yourselves, young women, do not make yourselves vomit, for if you do, oh shock, oh horror, you may end up like me.' It was disgraceful that she had been invited and exceedingly foolish of the organisers not to see the damage that might be done to impressionable and potentially ill young women by her display. Yet it happened.

Although it was wrong to have invited the Princess, the organisers were driven by the way the media react to issues. To get coverage of anything important is exceedingly difficult. Get a royal in and you can be sure that the press will turn out. If you're lucky, the resulting coverage will include just a little about the issue you care about.

It seems to me that there are parallels between the marketing of the Royals and the marketing of any other product. What royal products are being sold in the popular press? Product No.1 was Good News About the Monarchy. After many lucrative years – ever since Crawfie, in fact – it has been discontinued. After a while supply exceeded demand and the value of Good News About the Monarchy went down. The press had to find a new product, and came up with Product No.2: Bad News About the Monarchy. For a while it has been very successful, but after so many column inches, so many books, even this is getting exhausted. Intrigue is now a commodity like washing up liquid or breakfast cereal. It gets boring even if wilder and wilder claims are made, and public appetite fades away. There will have to be a fresh product soon. Could the new line be republicanism? I suspect it could.

If any monarchist is interested, the respondents to Anne and Nick's *Good Morning* are the ones who seem to have it right. Get the press to shut up for a while and maybe you'll be able to salvage something for the Royals. But let them go on as they are, and we'll be a republic before the millennium.

ANDREW MORTON

PROSPECTS FOR THE FAMILY

1992 MARKED THE end of the monarchy as we know it. Of course, it has been often said that the monarchy is on its last legs. Queen Victoria was one of the first to point it out, back in the 1840s. Peel said it too. Although the issue has been discussed many times over the centuries, we are now at a turning point. The institutional underpinning which has long sustained the monarchy has now been eroded or gone its own way. In the past, social events at Buckingham Palace were matched by social events at Chatsworth and elsewhere. Today the aristocracy is a far more humble institution. Once the Church of England was paramount. Now it is just one church amongst many in a multi-denominational society. The Conservative Party once walked hand-in-hand with the monarchy. Then came the Thatcher years, and all un-reformed institutions were measured against the bench mark of value for money. People now look at the monarchy and ask why do we need it? Why do we pay for it? And what does it cost?

The monarchy also has to confront an even more pernicious problem. Despite Charles' occasional vision of a dynamic and doing monarchy the Royal Family appears to lack the will to continue. A whole generation of royals doesn't really want to be royal any more.

The move into Europe, and other international events, are also having an impact. In 50 years time we will be closer to Europe than we are to the Commonwealth. The independence of Australia will take place in ten years time and there is a continuing constitutional crisis in Canada. The tide of history is moving against the monarchy.

It has become a commonplace to blame the tabloid press, and particularly Rupert Murdoch, for the tribulations the House of Windsor has undergone during the last years. The argument usually runs that if the tabloids did not intrude into their private lives, the royals would be under less pressure, their private problems could be resolved and the cloak of mystique in which they are wrapped would remain intact. A closer look suggests that the 1980s were a decade of real change in the Royal Family. An unstable cocktail comprising four ingredients – the coming of age of a 'bulge' generation of young royals, the explosion in charity work, the flirtation with the entertainment industry and the federal structure of the royal households – effectively exploded the values which have underpinned the mythology surrounding the Royal Family for a century. Family members themselves became the unwitting architects of their own decline, performing a genteel striptease as they shed the veils of mystery before the TV cameras.

Indeed the 'Woganisation of the Windsors' was the striking outward sign of the malaise which afflicted the family. For decades the twin imperatives of the Victorian constitutionalist Walter Bagehot that the monarch is to be 'reverenced' and surrounded by an opaque 'mystique' had been the philosophical sheet anchor which justified the need for a dignified distance between the Crown and its subjects.

That anchor was thrown overboard as the younger royal generation were seduced by the siren song of television, soothed by the zephyrs of sycophants and the illusion of ratings success. The importance of this development, the freefall of the Royal Family into the realm of trivia, cannot be over-emphasised. Bagehot's ringing commandment: 'above all our royalty is to be reverenced, and if you begin to poke about it you cannot reverence it. Its mystery is its life. We must not let in daylight upon magic', had served as the text for every monarch this century, including the present Queen who learnt her Bagehot in twice weekly visits to Sir Henry Marten, the Vice-Provost of Eton.

In the first decades of her reign the young monarch applied these teachings consistently, for example allowing television full access to the ceremonial aspects of the royal round, the weddings, the investiture of the Prince of Wales and so on, but drawing a veil over the private corners of royal life.

Programmes such as Huw Weldon's admirable *Royal Heritage* used the medium to *inform* the public about the monarchy rather than just *entertain*. Daylight was briefly allowed in when her then press secretary, Sir William Heseltine convinced the Queen to allow TV cameras to film the Royal Family *in situ*. The resulting documentary, called *Royal Family*, was the hit of 1969, showing royalty with a human face and a sense of humour. Even that fleeting glimpse of life in the goldfish bowl met stiff resistance within the Palace. After the documentary was screened the Queen's then private secretary Sir Michael Adeane, mindful of Bagehot's strictures, observed: 'We can no longer pretend. The Royal Family must now stand or fall on their own merits.'

Twenty years on, the architect of that radical departure from the past acknowledged that the original decision may have devalued the currency of monarchy by encouraging the unremitting small change of media interest. In a lecture on Sir Robert Menzies, Sir William, who became the Queen's private secretary, admitted: 'Are they themselves to blame in some degree by admitting the TV camera to their private lives for the making of the *Royal Family* film? The argument then was that the family appeared in the press as unreal, cardboard figures – no happy mean between the court circular with its quaint archaisms and the messiness of the gossip columns.'

It was not until after the wedding of the Prince and Princess of Wales in 1981 that the curtain of mystery was torn asunder, a process which has made royalty virtually synonymous with show business. It is perhaps appropriate that Prince Edward, as the first member of the first family ever to work in the commercial world, chose to enter the theatre, as a production assistant for Andrew Lloyd Webber's Really Useful Company.

The likes of Michael Parkinson, Selina Scott and of course Terry Wogan queued up to interview the Royal Family, coyly discussing their private lives whilst berating the tabloid press for their excesses. 'At one time it seemed that Buckingham Palace had been swapped for Television Centre, such was the parade of producers and directors discussing ideas for programmes', recalls one senior BBC executive. 'It was not all one way traffic. There were ideas from the Palace which we actually turned down.'

The Windsors, particularly the younger royals, conspired in the selling of their only asset – the mystique of their royalness in order to raise money for their charities. Again this points to a change in royal tradition where charitable concerns took precedence over civic duties.

Thus the famous Sir Alastair Burnet documentary on the Prince and Princess of Wales delicately inquired into their private lives, not their public concerns. There is no doubt about the popularity of royal TV shows – but that is not the point. The decision to appear on what the American academic Marshall MacLuhan called the 'hot medium' of television for no other reason than to entertain, strikes at the heart of the ideological framework which sustains the monarchy and essentially defines the difference between Joan Collins and Princess Diana. The younger generation of the Royal Family, with no intervention from wiser heads, saw little amiss with the constant uncritical, adulatory television coverage of their hobbies and their lives. The shallow applause of TV ratings was accepted in exchange for the deeper springs of reverence and mystery which are the last defence of the Royal Family against the pressures of the modern world.

This corrupting process is two way. In the studio, hardened interviewers were reduced to simpering sycophants while television's hallowed principles of independence and integrity were left on the cutting room floor as the Windsors were allowed effective editorial control over their programmes – a privilege denied the White House and Downing Street. Prince Charles for example vetoed scenes from the final version of the Burnet documentary which showed Princess Diana in the swimming pool at Highgrove.

The nadir of this haphazard policy was the Royal Knockout

Tournament in 1987 which embodied the inexorable drift from constitutional certainties within the monarchy. Prince Edward, fresh from his bruising encounter with the Royal Marines, used a television idea way past its sell-by date which combined royals with showbiz and sporting stars in a series of rather juvenile games based on a medieval theme. The sight of the Duchess of York, her voice hoarse with yelling, racing round the soggy turf like a sixth former or a grinning Duke of York hurling plastic fruit at his wife did little to burnish the dignity of the Crown. When ex-King Farouk of Egypt coined the *bon mot* that by the end of the century there would be only five royal houses, spades, diamonds, hearts, clubs and Windsor – he did not mean that they were to be the jokers in the pack. As one member of the Royal Family admitted following this very public debacle: 'If we carry on at this rate we will be like a firework, making a spectacle for a short time and then phut . . . gone.'

So during the 1980s, a decade of change, the trusted medium of television had its news and features agenda effectively set by Buckingham Palace. Therefore any television debate about the monarchy was defined by the Palace. As a result you could count on the fingers of one hand the number of serious discussion programmes made by either the BBC or ITN. Indeed there is nothing to choose between the BBC's uncritical coverage of the Royal Family during the 1980s and the relationship between *Pravda* and the Communist Party during the Brezhnev years.

Whilst television produced unbalanced, uncritical and trivial coverage of the Royal Family – often with their connivance – the tabloids were fulfilling their normal role of focusing on the 'human interest' angle of the monarchy. Their fashions, their marriages, their hobbies were all grist to that particular mill with the occasional feeding frenzy thrown in. If television is relatively trusted by people and has the ear of the establishment, the tabloids are akin to a seventeenth century mob. In between TV and the tabloids, the broadsheets, whose role is to address the 'public importance' issues abdicated their responsibilities. They allowed television and the tabloids to set the news agenda, so that debate was confined to the length of Diana's hemlines or so-called tabloid intrusion. Indeed, the *Independent* newspaper made their lack of royal coverage a selling point. There was little, if any, serious analysis of the role of the monarchy in modern society.

If the media was not changing, society was. When the Queen ascended the throne in 1953 some three out of ten people believed that she could claim direct descent from God. Few would concur nowadays. In the decade of Thatcherism every institution, from the National Health Service to the education system, has been measured by its value for money. The culture of financial utility inevitably extended to the monarchy. Yet while society was changing, the monarchy was buoyed in its complacency by a mass media content to peddle the fairytale image of the Royal Family whilst ignoring any discussion about the reforms necessary for the future health of the institution.

The mass media, particularly television, has performed a disservice to the sovereign over the last decade by fumbling its traditional role as a conduit, acting as a weathervane of the public mood and as an interface between the ruling establishment and the people. Instead the Queen has been in danger of suffocating under a barrage of media bromides when a bracing dose of reality could well have alerted her to the fact that public respect for the institution she has served for 40 years was rapidly diminishing.

It was a mood I first detected when I discussed my book on the Royal Family's wealth in the autumn of 1989. I was rather shocked by the suppressed anger and bitterness felt towards the Royal Family, its behaviour and its financial privileges, when I talked about the wealth of the Windsors during radio phone-ins and other forums of debate. At that time this undercurrent of public resentment was largely ignored by the mass media. Indeed when the Liberal Democrat MP Simon Hughes first introduced a bill which included modest proposals to tax the Queen he was curtly dismissed as a left-wing republican.

Yet away from the metropolitan movers and shakers, there

was a gradual fracturing of the historic compact between the sovereign and her subjects. The Windsor Castle fire was the turning moment. While media coverage was largely sympathetic, accepting the decision by Peter Brooke, the Heritage Secretary, that the taxpayer should pay for renovations, the public was in no mood to agree. A television phone-in poll produced 30,000 calls saying that the Queen should not only pay for the repairs but also pay tax. It was an intolerant almost ugly atmosphere of indignation that was reflected in newspaper postbags, radio phone-ins and elsewhere. The ghost of Mrs T finally handbagged the institution she had always protected.

(As a side note it might be argued that the Royal Family's hardships are a result of their failure to follow the lessons of history. The British aristocracy have survived far more effectively than their European counterparts because they have adapted to changed circumstances in society. While much diminished, the aristocracy is nonetheless a potent class in modern society – the *Sunday Times* list of the richest people in Britain notes that old money still dominates. Unfortunately change has not been a hallmark of this reign. Not only has the Queen resisted any attempts at reform, she has ensured that the monarchy has actually extended its fiscal privileges during the period.)

At the same time the institutions which traditionally underpinned the monarchy – the Church of England, the aristocracy and even the Conservative Party – have either declined or changed ideological tack. So when the tide of opinion turned there was little to stop the House of Windsor taking a pounding. The events of 1992 took a jackhammer to the carefully constructed carapace of myth and illusion surrounding the monarchy. It was a year when the British public awoke from their dream, a dream unnaturally prolonged by a media, particularly television, that has been content to administer chloroform to the national psyche.

Since then television, the broadsheets and the tabloids have devoted much attention to the future of the monarchy. For the first time in a generation, the monarchy has been taken seriously by serious people in Parliament, in public life and in the media. This debate is healthy not just for the monarchy but also for democracy.

RICHARD HOLME

DO WE NEED A HEAD OF STATE?

DO WE NEED a head of state at all? Let me proceed in a way perhaps unfamiliar and uncongenial to the British audience – by cross-cultural comparison. There are 62 plus democracies in the world, defined crudely as those countries that hold regular elections. I include in that total Russia. (I do not include the other states of the CIS simply because I am not sufficiently *au fait* with the latest developments.) Every one has a head of state, either a president or a constitutional monarch. In 25 of them the head of state is also the head of government, sometimes in a system of checks and balances like the United States, sometimes as in France with a hybrid system, and sometimes in South America, for instance, in what we might, by British standards, call an excessively 'hands-on' type of presidency.

There are nine constitutional monarchies including Britain, plus all the Commonwealth constitutional monarchies which spring from the British tradition – Australia, Canada, New Zealand plus Barbados and smaller Commonwealth states. The other constitutional monarchies are Belgium, Denmark, Japan, Luxembourg, Malaysia – where there is a rotating sultanship – Netherlands, Norway, Spain, and Sweden; then there is Jordan, where there are elections and the head of state is a monarch, but I do not think the country could possibly be defined as a conventional constitutional monarchy.

So the norm is that there is a head of state in countries that hold elections. We should ask ourselves why that is – what jobs there are to be done and what symbolism there is to be

116

expressed. Let me review the tasks of a head of state in summary. For the British head of state, but also generally for presidents in prime-ministerial systems, there is the job described by the constitutionalist Sir Ivor Jennings as to consult or be consulted, to encourage, and to warn. That seems a good idea, when you think of the loneliness of the person at the apex of power, the Prime Minister. As the saying in Boston has it about the Cabots and the Lodges (the Lodges speak only to God), so on the same basis, to whom does the Prime Minister speak? Well at least he has a head of state to speak to, to consult with, to be encouraged by, someone who potentially can warn him too, although we don't know much about that. We now know in retrospect that King George V, for instance, was quite free with his warnings to his Prime Ministers, but we do not know what form warnings take from Queen Elizabeth who has seen so many Prime Ministers come and go. There is then the role of constitutional legitimation, of signing bills, of confirming, as it were, that the acts of the executive are indeed legal and constitutional. There is the job of representation, both at home and abroad. The job of representation at home is perhaps particularly important symbolically, as a way of expressing national feelings at times of tragedy or times of celebration. This links to the issue of personification – the personification of the nation as a whole. Recently I wrote down all the names that we use in Britain to express the nation – particularly complicated because we have several nations within this polity. We have 'state' (state education, state secrets, we even have the state 1921 Liquor Act); we have 'public' (public accounts, public order, public trustees, public enquiry, public records); we have 'national' (as in national health, national savings, national parks, national galleries, national anthems); we have 'British' (as in British Broadcasting, British Railways); or we have 'royal' (as in Royal Air Force, Royal Navy, Royal Mail, and the more directly royal such as Her Majesty's Customs and so on). I think that this diverse spread of terms is an expression of something that troubles us in Britain. It comes partly from our constitutional confusion. We find difficulty in finding ways of talking about things that are ours as a whole, that cannot (or should not) be reduced to the temporary shifts of partisan government.

There is generally a sort of public relations function which the head of state performs, a spokesperson role. And then there is the role of contextual conscience for the nation. If you are looking for analogues here, the role that Richard von Weizacker has played in the Federal Republic of Germany has been most impressive; he has been a voice divorced from government but an eloquent voice, of national awareness and conscience, particularly in recent times with the rise of racial attacks. His has been another voice of moral authority for the country, if you like. The role that Mary Robinson is playing in the Irish Republic is a very similar role, an expression of the awareness of the moral nation.

Finally there is the symbolism. To what extent does the head of state symbolise the totality – all of us? This is particularly complicated in the United Kingdom because we have the division, a strong historical, cultural division, and political division between Scotland, Wales, England and Northern Ireland. It is a common complaint in other parts of the United Kingdom that there is a very English-dominated version of who 'us' and 'we' are. It is no coincidence that the British head of state, the British monarch, has gone to endless pains to have Princes of Wales, Dukes of Cornwall, and houses in Balmoral. It is a way, at least on the part of the British head of state, of trying to demonstrate and build some sense of *e pluribis unum*.

So most countries have a head of state and I do not find it at all difficult to think that there should be a head of state.

The question is, 'What sort of head of state do you want?' I would say that you do not want one that is mysterious. You will remember that the great thing about the medieval monarch was mystery. I do not believe in mystery because mystery is about the divine connection which I also do not believe in and which we have not entirely got out of our system – that somehow the monarch is there grace of courtesy of the Almighty. So I do not believe in the mystery, I am in favour of transparency. At the same time I do believe in dignity. I think there is a need for whoever the head of state is whether it is a

Mary Robinson, or Her Majesty the Queen, for dignity to be attached to the office because that is part of our self-respect. This does not mean pomp; it does not mean elaborately otiose forms of ceremony, but it does mean dignity. I think that the head of state must be genuinely constitutional – part of the constitution, symbol of the constitution, guardian of the constitution – and *not* a substitute for the constitution which is too often the way we look at the British monarch.

Thirdly, clearly the head of state has to be apolitical and totally divorced from party politics. This is particularly important for Britain, because we have one of the most partisan and adversarial political cultures in the world, where most questions of public interest are first defined in terms of party interest. It is very difficult to find a place on which to stand to arrive at public-interest definitions, hence again the importance of Charter 88.

So, as far as I am concerned, I therefore believe that we need a head of state, and a constitutional monarch. I do not believe that one can throw one's history out. We are partly made by our history, even as we move on to the hopes for our future. This is a continuum for all societies. Although there may come great crises at which people seek a historical disjunction, I think that you have to have an exceptionally good reason for one, and so I am persuaded that if we could have a fully constitutional monarch we should have one.

Having said this, the executive prerogative should be made far more accountable, within the normal system of government, and reviewable by the judiciary. I am particularly exercised by the fact that the monarch has within her personal prerogative two powers that I do not believe that he or she should be expected to exercise. One is the power not merely to appoint, but to choose the Prime Minster, and secondly, the power to accede to or refuse a dissolution of Parliament. The first is not a big problem as long as you have single-party government and parties elect their own leaders, because it is then clear on whom the monarch calls. The British electorate, however, vote consistently for a multi-party system. And when we have electoral reform, which we shall at some point, we will almost certainly have more coalitions in this country. Even with first-past-the-post voting we may have no overall majority for one party. The head of state could be put in a political position, of choosing which party leader to call in which order and, what time to allow for negotiations. The right of a Prime Minister to go to the Palace and ask for a dissolution will then become *itself* part of whether parliaments are going to settle down to coalition or whether they are going to try to do an end-run around it and cause an election before a parliament is fully exhausted. So I think there is a great case for throwing back into Parliament, as far as you possibly can, the obligation itself by resolution within a fixed-term parliament to decide when it is exhausted, to positively vote for an end of the parliament, rather than the Prime Minister being able to threaten his own end-run to the Palace.

I also think, by the same token, that the more one can take the Crown out of the choice of Prime Minister the better; there may be a role for a negotiator, what is called a *formateur* on the Continent. But it is time to recognise now, ahead of time, that if we were to have a hung parliament in Britain, it is very likely, because of the wish of Buckingham Palace to avoid being involved in politics precisely for the motive that I am ascribing to them (to be above and outside politics) that the Palace would take a very conservative and minimalist view of the possibilities of there being a negotiated coalition; they would take the *least* adventurous view of what could be achieved. I think that might mean that the country might miss a great reforming opportunity.

JAMES CORNFORD

IT'S THE CIVIL SERVICE, SILLY

> . . . whereas all these other constitutions have created an office
> (the presidency) and invested it with certain powers, in Britain
> the converse obtains. The office is primeval, and the historical
> role of the constitution has been to whittle away its powers and
> transfer them to other offices.
>
> S E Finer

THIS IS A clear definition of the historical constitution. While
many powers of the Crown have been transferred to other
offices, substituted by statutory provision or controlled by
convention, certain powers remain with the monarch – and
more importantly the Prime Minister or the government – and
are not subject to parliamentary control or judicial oversight.
The Prime Minister and government depend on the support of
a majority in the House of Commons, but prerogative powers
can be and are freely used to maintain the authority of the
government, through patronage and other means.

The personal powers of the monarch remain significant in
two related matters: the appointment of the Prime Minister
and the granting of a dissolution of Parliament. This is not a
problem when one party wins a clear majority of seats in the
Commons following a general election. By convention, the
monarch sends for the leader of that party to form a
government. The difficulties begin when there is no majority:
the monarch's decision as to whom to invite to form a
government may have a significant effect on the outcome,
especially where the appointed Prime Minister is able to ask

for a dissolution of Parliament and a further election at the time most helpful to his or her party.

It is unlikely that this difficulty would be overcome by the replacement of an hereditary head of state with an elected one. The essential issue is whether the head of state's decision is acceptable to politicians and the public.

There are a number of ways to avoid the difficulty of a head of state making decisions which confer partisan advantage. The question could be thrown to the House of Commons and the parties could sort it out for themselves. The head of state or monarch would then appoint as Prime Minister whoever was elected by the Commons. Secondly the power of dissolution could be removed from the monarch (and the Prime Minister) by establishing fixed term parliaments. Dissolutions would only be possible if the Government lost a vote of confidence, if at all.

Provisions to this effect are included in the *Constitution of the United Kingdom* drafted by the Institute for Public Policy Research in 1991.

As Graham Allen, Labour's current spokesperson on constitutional affairs, has pointed out, the most important prerogative powers of the Crown are exercised by the Prime Minister and other ministers, and they are outside democratic control. These powers cover the conduct of international relations, including treaties; much of the conduct of economic policy; the exercise of patronage, including public appointments; honours and life peerages; the control and management of the civil service and the security services.

The essential point about the exercise of these powers is that insofar as they require parliamentary approval it is only *after* the event. The extent to which these powers can be controlled by the courts also remains doubtful and is an area of conflict. These powers therefore confer much greater freedom of action on the government than when it is acting upon statutory powers provided by Parliament and subject to judicial review. All governments require some degree of discretionary power: that enjoyed by British governments is exceptionally wide.

The civil service provides an important if undramatic

example. There are serious questions to be asked about the civil service and its relationship to ministers. The established tradition is that the civil service is neutral as between parties, though it is widely recognised that departments do have views or settled policies about the matters for which they are responsible. It is understood that civil servants, collectively and individually, do in fact exercise significant and sometimes decisive influence on policy. Given their numbers, permanence, knowledge and skills it would be surprising if this were not the case. The undue influence of the civil service has given rise to a long running debate: critics of both left and right have argued that their policies have been frustrated.

In constitutional terms however, the civil service is subordinate to ministers and unprotected. A former head of the civil service has declared that Crown servants have no separate or independent constitutional status. They owe their allegiance to the Crown, and for all practical purposes that means the ministers of the day. It remains doubtful whether they enjoy the accepted contractual rights of employees, although the decision of the courts in the GCHQ case implies that they do. However that may be, their terms and conditions of employment are made by Order in Council under prerogative powers and are not subject to parliamentary approval. Civil servants therefore have no effective protection against ministers. There are no clear rules on what is appropriate conduct or what work they may properly be asked to undertake. There is a convention that civil servants cost the opposition's manifesto commitments before a general election. If this is a legitimate activity it is difficult to see where the line is to be drawn on neutrality. Incidents like the Westland affair and the Matrix Churchill case reveal a degree of political involvement – and a willingness not merely to be economical with the truth but actively to mislead Parliament – which does not conform to textbook niceties.

The prerogative basis of the civil service also means that governments can undertake radical and far reaching reforms of the administrative machine without the need for parliamentary consultation or approval.

The position of the civil service needs to be put on a statutory basis and Parliament should be given a much larger say in the organisation of central government. This may not be a glamorous or exciting reform but I think it is much more relevant to the good government of Britain than the means by which our head of state is chosen.

JACK STRAW

ABOLISH THE ROYAL PREROGATIVE

THE ROYAL PREROGATIVE has no place in a modern western democracy.

My preference is for a slimmed-down, Scandinavian-style constitutional monarchy, rather than a republic. But whatever system we end up with, it must be one which is transparent in its operation, and in its distribution of power. It must have the explicit consent of the British people. What people get, must be what they see.

Much of the basic law of the United Kingdom is to be found in statute. And there is plenty of description about how the rest of the constitution works – not least in Erskine May's *Parliamentary Practice*. The depiction of Britain's constitution as 'unwritten' has always been a misnomer. What is distinctive about the British arrangement is not that it is unwritten, but that only part of our constitutional arrangement has ever been formally endorsed by Parliament. The rest derives from the Royal Prerogative.

The history, first of representative government, then of democratic government in this country can be charted through the history of the Royal Prerogative. Each establishment of rights by Parliament has involved, by definition, a corresponding restriction upon the Royal Prerogative. Notable examples are the Bill of Rights of 1688, the Act of Settlement of 1700–1, the Succession to the Crown Act of 1707; and in this century, the Parliament Acts of 1911 and 1949.

The 'rest' is not a trivial remainder, but the heart of our system of government. As Erskine May records, 'The prerogatives

125

of the Crown, in connection with Parliament, are of paramount importance. The legal existence of Parliament results from the exercise of Royal Prerogative'. [21st ed. p 89]. The Queen appoints the archbishops and bishops. 'All titles of honour are the gift of the Crown. To a Queen's writ, also, the House of Commons owe their election as representatives of the people. To these fundamental powers are added others of scarcely less importance', which includes the declaration of war, the signing of treaties, and much of the executive power of ministers.

Accountability of the executive is fundamental to any democracy. Where power is based not upon statute but upon the Royal Prerogative it is this accountability which suffers. The honours system plays a crucial – and often brutal – role in the exercise of partisan political power. As unelected quangos have multiplied, and replaced so many functions previously exercised by elected councillors, so the honours system has been used to reward those – for example in health authorities – who have done their ministers' bidding, who have kept their mouths shut in the face of scandals (from fiddled computer contracts to deaths on the wards), and who have always put the most favourable interpretation upon waiting lists. The coincidence between large scale donations to the Tory Party, and the receipt of serious honours like knighthoods and peerages is too stark to ignore (and serves only to show up the total inadequacy of the vetting system).

Yet, because honours flow from the royal pen, no question about their award is allowed in Parliament, save by substantive motion. So ministers are in practice wholly unaccountable for the exercise of this considerable power. The changes announced recently by the Prime Minister do not alter this. The distribution of lower grade honours like OBEs may change a little, but that of serious honours will not.

Most of the discussion about the Royal Prerogative centres on the way in which it has been used as a smoke-screen by ministers to obfuscate the use of power for which they are insufficiently accountable. That is entirely right. As the Labour National Policy Forum paper *A New Agenda for Democracy* makes clear, this has to change. 'Massive power is exercised by executive decree without accountability to Parliament, and sometimes even without its knowledge', it says. So the paper proposes that the declaration of war and the ratification of treaties must both, explicitly, be a matter for Parliament.

Other proposals in the paper, for a bill of rights, for a freedom of information act, for the replacement of the House of Lords by an elected second chamber, and in respect of the reform of the judiciary, taken together would involve the single greatest reduction in the use by ministers of the Royal Prerogative.

What has been insufficiently discussed in the past is the effect of the Royal Prerogative on the position of the monarchy itself. Ministers have been insufficiently accountable for their executive decisions as a result of their use of prerogative powers. By the same token, the monarchy has been scarcely accountable at all for its conduct of this crucial institution at the heart of our constitutional arrangements. Members of Parliament are not permitted to question the conduct of the sovereign. In my experience the Clerks at the Table are quicker to alert the chair of possible transgressions of this rule than almost any of the other rules of debate.

This rule has had a paradoxical consequence. Designed to maintain the dignity of the monarchy and shield the institution and its holder from partisan political comment, it actually leaves it unaware of the true state of both parliamentary and public feeling. It makes the monarch more vulnerable, not less. Parliament is denied one of its roles as the mouthpiece of public concern and the barometer of public opinion. I believe the ban on criticism inside Parliament also leads, among politicians, to a taboo on criticism outside Parliament.

The Palace, insulated from day-by-day parliamentary criticism makes the enormous, but understandable error, of believing that silence means consent. Criticism, though painful, keeps institutions, and the individuals who serve them, on their toes. It enables them to adapt and survive. But the ban and the taboo have meant that a lot of debates that should have taken place in Parliament on the role of the last twentieth century monarchy have had to take place outside, not least through the prurient and unacceptable proxy of intrusion into the Royal Family's private life.

The extent of latent parliamentary concern about the current state of the monarchy only came home to me after I made a speech in January 1993 suggesting that it had to change. To my great surprise, a large number of Conservative MPs came up to me and endorsed what I had said. To my even greater surprise, not a single Tory MP sought to exploit my speech for Party advantage during Prime Minister's questions over the following weeks. Had No. 10, or the Tory whips, believed that there was any mileage in giving support to the Royal Family and bashing me, they would have organised it instantly . On this occasion, however, the silence was deafening – and it indicated broad assent for what I had been saying.

If my assessment of the mood of many in the Conservative Party is correct then it means that we should able to conduct a debate about the future of the monarchy which will not fissure along party lines. That I believe is essential. The views I express are personal, not party.

I believe there is now a widespread understanding that things cannot remain as they are. The monarchy might be good for tourism, but it is bad for citizenship in the late twentieth century. I am not in favour of the complete upheaval which a republic would bring. But we do need a new Act of Settlement, to establish the Crown and the monarchy in a more modern form. Over time – and it is bound to take time – we should aim for a situation where all powers exercised by the executive, and by the monarch, are based upon statute, sometimes (as with voting systems) reinforced by direct decisions of the electorate through referenda. Only then could we 'concentrate the national mind on the hard decisions of the distribution of power,' in the way that *A New Agenda for Democracy* suggests.

Joe Rogaly observed in the *Financial Times* on May 18th 1993 that the constitutions of Europe's northern monarchies 'specify exactly what their kings and queens may do'. So should we. The quality of our democracy would benefit – but so, by the by, would the quality of life of members of the Royal Family. Far too much has been dumped on them; far too much has been expected of them that is beyond the capacity of any family to achieve, especially in an age of total mass communication.

One traditional, but I think powerful, case for a constitutional monarchy is that it is easier, in the non-political personage of a sovereign, to represent the notion of the state, and the people, as requiring a loyalty separate and distinct from that due to the government of the day. Civil servants are reminded that they owe duties to the Crown above and beyond those which they owe to ministers. I think that any new, and explicit constitutional statement needs to take account of this and strengthen the constitutional integrity of the civil service.

RICHARD HOGGART

RANK ATTITUDES

WHENEVER I THINK about that complicated mix and gelling in British attitudes towards rank, show, money, royalty and the *lares et penates* of suburban life, two images swim into view, one several decades old, the other recent. But they hang together, sadly.

The older one is of a certain Lady Docker, the wife of Sir Bernard Docker who was chairman of the huge BSA (British Small Arms Ltd) conglomerate in Birmingham not long after the war. Lady Docker was monumentally vulgar, like a retired chorus girl who had married into money and meant to flaunt it. She rode in a gold-plated Daimler and sought acceptance in high places. I do not know if she ever mixed with royalty but below that level she was accepted. Except, oddly but to their credit, by the Rainiers of Monaco who found her ostentatious antics too hard to bear.

She was the glittering pinnacle of a triangle. One leg of it was the tabloid press who rightly guessed that their readers would swallow this glossy coarseness by the bucket load and so gave Lady Docker massive attention.

Little did those readers know that the other leg of the triangle, Sir Bernard himself, was presiding over the collapse of his industrial empire. Not enough R and D, not enough attention to new design, not enough sales-initiative. The BSA motor-bike, as I knew from the last war, was a fine machine. Like the rest of British motor-cycle production it lost to the Japanese. And thus the miserable collapse went on. Sir Bernard ran a crumbling complex at the heart of British manufacturing;

his wife spent money like confetti; the workers swallowed all the silly, glossy tattle of the tabloids – and lost their jobs in thousands. It was a microcosm of so many things that were and are wrong with Britain.

My second picture is less striking but no less potent. Not very long ago I was queuing at the check-out in our Sainsbury's behind two obviously middle-class women in early middle age. One of them turned to the other and said simply, without preamble: 'Isn't it a *pity* about Charles and Di.' Members of their local tennis club? Neighbours in their Queen Anne executive-housing close? Neither, of course; but the heir apparent had been seamlessly absorbed into the middle-class suburban myth. 1992. We don't change.

That pattern: royalty seen as part of a phoney middle-class family – many of whom thrive in places like Farnham much as they ever did; that love of money, show, rank; that sheer attachment to the constituents of a saccharine, small-minded snobbery; the popular press's shameful role in feeding all those attitudes; and the sententious voices of the lackeys – some editors of broadsheets, some lords and other parliamentarians fond of quoting Bagehot, some heads of Oxbridge colleges. All these things help sustain an institution which has outlived its usefulness and can only be propped up by sentimentality, fawning, misguided history, self-interest and muddled thinking.

I tell those two anecdotes because they illustrate a major fact: that most British people are not ready intellectually or, more importantly, imaginatively to have done with the monarchy. It would be silly to let our blood boil about this and self-indulgent to accept it 'for others'. We can each of us, though, run up a little flag in the meantime. For what this is worth I have refused three invitations to Buckingham Palace and one royally bestowed honour. No histrionics, just a polite refusal.

I want to say something about patronage and heritage. We all know and are properly impressed by the Princess Royal's transmogrification from a royal goose to a royal swan, especially in her work for the Save the Children Fund.

131

But in general my experience of royal patronage is of snobbery – and jobbery. I remember more than one call to the Arts Council from disgruntled clients who did not hesitate to point out that their patron HRH something or other, was particularly anxious that their grant be increased. Were we meant to bow low at this instance of royal interest or shake in our shoes before, in either or both cases, handing over the money?

For at all levels the British are besotted with titles. When I complained that the Royal Shakespeare Company governors were given nothing to do at their quarterly meetings I was told that for many people being a governor alone was regarded as a sufficient honour and that hence many people – 'even people who are already titled' – let it be known that they would welcome the elevation.

Similarly, people will actually ask to be nominated for honorary degrees. Most universities look around for some sprig of royalty to become their chancellor. To its credit the new university of Leicester was one of the first to shun that practice. It sought and obtained a great scientist, Lord Adrian. That is admirable academic democracy.

So it all goes on. I am virtually convinced that the House of Lords can have a useful role to play these days. I am entirely sure nonetheless that the existence of hereditary peers is an inexcusable hangover. The fact that it remains is a tribute to that network of snobberies and sentimentalities I have been describing; and to that ingrained lethargy which the British like to call tolerance. So it all goes on and will go on for some time yet.

It is, in these days, buttressed by tourism and by the image of Britain promoted by the British Tourist Board. A film set, a nostalgic, television-type, costume drama: which most tourists do lap up, certainly. I sometimes think of offering another set of pictures to those who are not taken in; a tour round Hull, Hunslet, Halifax to have a look at 'the people of England who have not spoken yet', those who have received little more than 'the enormous condescension of history'. And a final look at a modern suburbia; say, Fleet in Hampshire, pure Waitrose country, where wife-swapping also is said to thrive.

So there we are; it is bound to be a long, slow haul. Meanwhile, we can clear away some favourite counter arguments to change. Above all, that which says: 'You will need a figurehead'. True, probably. 'But what you are likely to get in this country is a worn-out politician, a tired trade union boss, an elderly aristocratic hack. Better the devil. . .' True again; but this response is precisely an extension of that sad substitute for thought which I have been describing, this assumption that a replacement for the monarch would be likely, would almost have to, come from that tired, old, routine procession. Unless we took better thought.

It would be one good sign of change, an indication that we were ready for change, that we thought quite differently. A pleasant game, that, to think of possible people outside the expected conventional names as possible presidents. Other countries have found non-executive presidents who are dignified, wise, demotic. Have a good think. Having just read her very impressive new book on metaphysics and morals I put forward, as a first shot, Iris Murdoch.

So what should be done to reduce this weight of privilege, patronage, snobbisms? There are some practical steps of varying difficulty. Number one would be to move towards abolishing hereditary peerages. Number two would be the reform of the public schools.

The really difficult steps are more long-term and trickier; they are, by education, by writing, by irony and comedy to reduce the need in so many people for this sentimental pabulum, and to shame out of their awful flattery of people with these attitudes so many who should know better – journalists of all persuasions and levels, members of both Houses of Parliament, all those 'gatekeepers of opinion' whose gates haven't been oiled or inspected for death-watch beetle for generations. So that it eventually becomes a matter of self-respect to avoid talking about the monarchy as an institution 'giving innocent pleasure to the people'. Urgh! Or to refuse to talk about it as a 'symbol of our heritage'. That's not the enormous condescension of history but the continuing condescension of those who at present blindly prop up this foolish remnant, this sentimental pacifier.

Meanwhile, we can cheer ourselves up by recognising that a fair number of people at all levels do not succumb, are not taken in, 'aren't as daft as all that'.

BILLY BRAGG

ENGLAND MADE ME, TOO

I RECENTLY READ an article about how many countries there are in the world. This is a bit of a puzzler as there are so many definitions of what constitutes a 'country' as opposed to a 'territory', or a 'protectorate', or a 'nation'. One of the more interesting questions posed was whether or not Scotland was a country. Perhaps it was merely a province of a larger country, the UK? The author obviously identified England so strongly with the UK that it did not occur to him to ask the same question about us. If Scotland is merely a province, then by the same definition England is not a country either. This illustrates the blind-spot the English seem to have when wearing their 'British' hat – when we refer to Britain we often mean England and vice versa.

Where does Englishness end and Britishness begin? And why are the English so confused about their national identity? The Welsh and Scots are happy to sport flowers in their lapels on St David's or St Andrew's Day but how often do the English wear roses on St George's Day? Are we too embarrassed to indulge in outbursts of national celebration or do we not want to draw attention to the fact that we have an identity that is separate from 'British'?

The monarch is central to our notion of being British. Our national anthem is not a glorious song about the nice country we inhabit but a hymn calling for supernatural intervention to ensure the longevity of our monarch. We sing 'Long to reign over us' because the presence of the monarch allows England to continue its favourite dream – the Dream of Empire. Once we had power over our own destiny and the fortunes of other nations. Now all we have left is an unhealthy obsession with empty symbols of that power. Amongst these is the title 'British', which we English wear like an old soldier's uniform discovered in the attic.

While dreaming this imperial dream we have lost touch with our true identity and the peculiar things that make us English.

To find the moment when we were discouraged to think of ourselves as anything but British, we must look into our own history, to those years just before the founding of the Empire. Before the colonisers could set out to enslave half the globe, the English themselves had to be disenfranchised. Their age old traditions had to be replaced with a single unifying ideal: Monarchy Culture. Before the Act of Union in 1707, 'Britain' was a term used rather like 'Scandinavia' is today. It signified a group of nations with close geographical links. Great Britain as we understand it came into being as a direct result of the restoration of the monarchy and the 'Glorious Revolution'. The years of the Commonwealth Republic, from 1649–60, had given a severe shock to the merchants and squires who were attempting to become the new ruling classes. During the Civil War and in the years that followed they had experienced what the English, given a few basic freedoms, were capable of. They were terrified. The Radicals in the Army, the Levellers and the Diggers – those first chaotic flowerings of utopianism in England – were all within the living memory of the men who laid foundations of the constitutional monarchy by inviting William of Orange to invade England in 1688.

Their problems had begun when Charles I was beheaded in Whitehall. With that revolutionary act, the Establishment lost much of its legitimacy in the eyes of the populace. It was as if the monarch had held totemic sway over the tribe and without it the demons of Reason were unleashed. The new ruling classes were swift to learn from this chastising experience and, after restoring the monarchy, immediately set about entrenching their power in a new United Kingdom of Great Britain. Until 1707 only the Welsh had referred to themselves as Britons and rightly so, as they were the heirs to the language and culture of the ancient Celtic people who gave their name to these islands. The English Establishment made 'being British' into a Protestant crusade and drew Lowland Scottish merchants away from the Jacobites by offering them access to the lucrative English market and a stake in the building of the Empire.

What happened to the English while this was going on? They got a new identity and became 'Anglo-Saxon'. This strange mongrelisation, first coined in the late seventeenth century as a linguistic term, needs examination. Obviously, as this is *Eng* – land, the Angles were prime candidates for inclusion. But what was the hyphen for? And why, from all the diverse groups that contributed to the cultural melting pot that was England in the Dark Ages, were the Saxons chosen? The Danes, the Celts and the Normans had all contributed to the English language, so why not Anglo-Norse or Anglo-Celt or Anglo-Norman? Was the choice anything to do with the fact that a Protestant Germanic dynasty had been installed on the throne? Claiming the Saxon as our racial type had the immediate effect of allying us with the north European Protestant states against Spain and France, the Catholic superpowers of the day.

Declaring ourselves to be Anglo-Saxons also served a domestic purpose. It devalued the Celtic tradition in England while simultaneously associating it with the Jacobites who represented a return to Catholicism and the pre-Civil War order. This has been an English trick ever since – identifying themselves by pointing out what they are not and thus neatly obscuring what they truly are.

So what do I see when I close my eyes and think of England? I can understand how the concept of Englishness often makes people uneasy. On the one hand there is the little Englander, who takes our geographical isolation from the Continent as a licence for xenophobia. On the other there is the Merrie Englander, who imagines a country full of Laura Ashley prints and morris dancers – a pastoral idyll that is still sought after, even though it never existed in the first place. My own feelings of Englishness are based not on patriotism or chauvinism, but on a sense of history, environment and identity.

The England that made me was one which had rejected reliance on charity in favour of a system which recognised the benefits of communal responsibility. In this England a deep sense of social justice contributed to the founding of the Welfare State, then perhaps the best of its kind in the world. The Welfare State was not introduced as a 'safety net' for the poor and weak. It was founded on the conviction that the provision of decent work, education, health care and housing are necessary to make a modern, industrial economy function properly. Today this seems to be something that our European partners recognise.

How revealing, then, that it is on this very principle that the Conservative Government has chosen to opt-out. They are the ones who cling hardest to the concept of United Kingdom sovereignty while resisting full integration into a United Europe. They fail to realise that the United Kingdom is a good example of how union between former enemies can lead to a sustained period of prosperity. And in any case a federal Europe in which states were united while remaining independent in internal affairs would be a looser arrangement than the one currently in force within the UK.

But the British establishment seems not to know how to work with other member states, just as it has lost the ability to do so with the peoples of Scotland and Wales, and I would add England. It does not want the direction of either the Union of Europe or the Union of Britain to be set by a democratically formulated consensus. To put it bluntly, the government would not always get its own way. Genuine European Union would mean that centuries of privilege, patronage and power would be diluted and devolved away from their hands. The old regime could begin to buckle and even its corroded bolt, the monarchy, could give way.

Queen Elizabeth is the last of her kind. Not because of the shortcomings of certain members of her family, but because of the way in which those who govern us have exploited our loyalty to the Queen for their own ends. When it comes to the crunch, and despite her best efforts she does not belong to us, she belongs to them. She is not the Queen of England. She is the

Queen of the Establishment. Her role in the unwritten constitution serves to legitimise its continued existence, its traditions and its goals. As we move towards integration with Europe, the challenge is not whether we should tear down the tacky remnants of the divine right of kings. It is to bring to an end the divine right of Etonians and their cronies to run this country of ours for themselves. This is what we are up against. We should not be misled by suggestions that pageantry and heritage are good for the tourist industry. We should remove the Crown from the insignia of our state and recover our rights. In the process we will be able to discover something more and positive about our identity.

It will be a struggle for the soul of England. It will have a dark side. There is no guarantee that the positive outcomes that I have evoked will win. But if Englishness is to be more than a cause for embarrassment (and very occasional pleasure) at Wembley Stadium or Lords, it will be because of a struggle joined by the majority of us in these islands who no longer accept that singing 'Rule Britannia' at the top of our voices gives us a place or a role in the world that we want.

CAROLINE ELLIS

A RIGHT LITTLE ROYALIST

1977: THE SILVER Jubilee is engraved on my memory. That was the year I found fame in the local press for my appearance in North Town Primary School's Easter Bonnet Parade. For I alone had the wit to create a replica of Queen Elizabeth's Crown: a huge and cumbersome concoction of cardboard, cotton wool and sticky-back plastic. A right little royalist.

That year, me and my sister Del (five years my junior) graced every street party and fête within a ten-mile radius of our home in matching long red, white and blue dresses with puffy sleeves, plastic union jacks clasped in our hands.

My last act of loyalty to the Crown was on the occasion of the Royal Wedding (Charles and Di's) when I performed 'God Save the Queen' on my new saxophone in the middle of our street to the delight of the neighbours.

I overdosed on monarchy at a young age. At the public school I attended from age thirteen, monarchy, state religion, snobbery and militarism all seemed to fuse into one. Compulsory school chapel each morning (evaded with much cunning), a headmaster obsessed with making his school fit for a Prince (he was convinced we were in the running to receive William), hundreds of uniformed 'sprogs' marching around the school grounds on a Tuesday afternoon practising with their rifles, prize-givings at which the likes of Lord Denning saw off 'those horrible comprehensives' to thunderous applause: the over-dose killed any penchant for all things monarchical.

These are the skeletons in my republican wardrobe. I am not alone. Most friends of around my age (I am 25) have similar experiences, if not of a stifling public school system, of a time when royalty was an inescapable and entertaining part of our landscape – a given. They still have their Silver Jubilee mugs, they remember the excitement of Charles and Di's wedding. 'It's great when you're little,' says Rachel, 22, now a republican (and a civil servant!) Black youngsters felt the same. Rashid, 25, comments: 'When I was growing up there was a fascination with the Jubilee and Royal Wedding. When my Dad said Benn was right to say the monarchy should be abolished, I thought – you evil man!' Even my best friend, Diamond, 24, organised a party for her little brother and his friends in their neighbourhood on the occasion of the Royal Wedding. Diamond puts this down to the spectacle of royalty, a spectacle she has long since outgrown.

Who knows what makes little royalists into republicans? For my sister it was partly being on the dole, and the mismatch between Royal Britain and the everyday struggles of friends who had been thrown out of their home. For most of us anti-monarchist stirrings formed part of a wider appreciation of the structures of power and the way that unwritten, archaic rules and institutions keep us subjects.

Only two of my peers I've interviewed said they favoured adherence to monarchy, though they said they didn't think about it much. Jane, 21, said it made her feel more patriotic. Her brother, Jon, 23 gave more grudging support finding the image of the Royals shallow. He thought some kind of continuity important: 'The fear of an elected President, is the fear of the unknown'. If these two are the exception to the rule and a generational gap in attitudes to the monarchy is indeed quite widespread, to what can it be attributed?

Every Christmas day there are unseemly wrangles in our living room about whether or not to listen to the Queen's broadcast. My mother usually wins: 'If we didn't have a monarchy, we would have to invent it! Just think what Thatcher would have been like if there had been no one above her'. But she also has a deeper attachment to the monarchy. She remembers my granddad, by no means a royalist, waking her up to tell her Prince Charles had been born and putting out a full Union Jack flag on royal occasions. The Coronation and the street parties which went with it are fondly remembered. 'It was like a fairy tale. I had a lovely book with pictures of the two little princesses and their long white socks and their corgis'. Today she thinks the monarchy still performs a vital role: 'Everybody feels they have got a part of them, that they belong to us all in some way. I would be distressed if there wasn't a King Charles III, we need our roots, our heritage.'

My father expresses similar views: 'I'm definitely in favour of a monarchy – someone above the political wrangling, infighting and pettiness. We need a titular head of state who can't be touched. It provides for continuity when you have prats like Thatcher or Major in power. I don't think discontent with the system is bound up with the monarchy, but perhaps I don't know enough. The case against the monarchy hasn't been made: they should be innocent until proven guilty.'

Their 'two little princesses' think themselves wiser. For my part, I cannot accept that the monarchy is a protection against tyranny, the events of the last fifteen years are proof enough of that. My sister has not bought this either, displaying a healthy degree of disrespect: 'What does the monarchy mean for me? It's all a load of crap really. Kill the corgis. Abolish headscarves and the green puffy jackets with the diamond stitching. Oh, and can we please not have Trooping the Colour on right in the middle of Saturday morning TV? But seriously, if we are going to keep the monarchy – and I don't see it being abolished – it should be reformed, they should buck up their ideas. The Queen is too old – she should retire.'

At least my parents' support for the monarchy has partly democratic premises: the monarchy seems to offer some kind of protection against the schemes and machinations of power-hungry politicians and the appalling vista of an elected and thus corruptible president. This view appears to be widely held. In the workshop on republicanism at the Monarchy Conference, Hilary Wainwright pointed out that for many, the Queen is seen as the ultimate guarantor of our civil liberties and of democracy itself. The miners' wives, for example, turned to the Queen for help in their campaign to save their pits.

I put this to Rachel: 'The monarchy irritates me. I do not believe you can have democracy with a non-elected head of state. I also think it's an abuse of people's money – the millions we spend on them every year. I want it abolished. I don't see how you can reform it. The Queen does bugger all and you wouldn't want her more involved in affairs of state. My parents are in favour of keeping the monarchy for similar reasons to yours. Mainly because they think a non-elected head of state is a safeguard against one-party control of the whole parliamentary system.' I ask her, why this difference in perspective? 'Maybe it has something to do with the legacy of World War II and Hitler and that this must never happen again. They think that somehow a monarchy strengthens us against this.'

Ian, 25, puts the generation gap down to a change in attitudes towards authority and institutions. 'When my parents think of the police, they think of them acting in the public good, whereas I'm more likely to think "they beat up black people don't they?" It's the same with the monarchy.' Is he prepared to humour those who, like his parents, place a lot of store on heritage and the monarchy as reflecting our national character? 'No! I really do think the monarchy affects our political culture. If ministers didn't have the Royal Prerogatives to hide behind, we might be able to make them more accountable. Of course we need other constitutional reforms. I think the whole monarchical system is holding us back – in our attitudes towards Europe, for example. So I would be prepared to sacrifice flag-waving sensibilities in favour of real democracy.'

The crucial distinction for me and my friends is that of subject and citizen. But is this mere sophistry? Diamond trained as a lawyer: 'In the US legal system cases are brought in the name of the people rather than the Crown. People are citizens rather than subjects.' Does this make a difference though? 'A Norwegian woman I met recently said she was amazed by her British peers – how apolitical they are, how indifferent they are to their rights compared to Norwegian society. So I think the monarchy adds to our complacency. It also keeps us in the dark about what really goes on, preventing us from knowing how ministers exercise their powers. It means we don't have open or accountable government.'

Diamond's parents, who consider themselves British-Ghanaian citizens, as opposed to 'English', don't have the same emotional bond to the monarchy as mine. 'My parents see the monarchy as just another example of the offensive anachronisms of life in this country and the "unreal" way in which the English view themselves.' I ask her if she thinks the existence of a monarchy, bound up in notions of nationhood, in some way serves to legitimise and reinforce little England-ism and – by extension – racism in this country. Indirectly perhaps, she replies, but the racists are denying the reality of their own history. 'Nationalists hark back to a homogenous view of Britishness or Englishness that never really existed. What about the Celts, the Normans, the Angles, the Saxons? What about all those different peoples who originally made up the British Isles? When the Welsh are asked if Prince Charles represents them, they say, NO.'

Rashid, who attended the Monarchy Conference, took issue with one speaker who thought that black people should engage with the monarchy and use it to put issues of importance to them on the agenda. 'The monarchy is at the pinnacle of an essentially autocratic system. One of the saddest things to me is that many working class people in this country have little idea of where power is or how it is exercised. Politicians collude in this ignorance. The monarchy deflects attention away from issues of power and distributive justice towards the soap opera of the institution itself. The monarchy underpins a system of haves and have-nots: not just in the economic or materialist sense, in a broader sense. I come from a world of have-nots. At school I was only dimly aware that other kids had parents who belonged to the professions, we had no contacts whatsoever. People say 'it's a small world'. It's not. It's a very large world, it's just that a small clique populates all our institutions. I am the first member of my family to go to university and I've now entered a profession so I can see it from both sides of the fence and it's a very tall fence.'

Rashid lives with Catherine, 28 – her family come from New Zealand. She is a republican herself, but her parents, especially her mother, are strong royalists: they think the monarchy represents the best of Britain's cultural traditions. 'New Zealand is like Britain 30 years ago. My parents look back to the early 50s as the ideal way of organising society – the monarchy reinforces those values. My generation on the other hand look more realistically at British society and they see a very diverse culture which the monarchy in no way personifies.'

A change in perceptions of all our institutions, the monarchy included, and of British exceptionalism has most definitely occurred in the last thirty years. A Gallup poll in February 1993 attempted to gauge some of these. While British men are thought to have become less emotionally repressed and better lovers than 20–30 years ago (hurrah to that) just about everything else has gone to the dogs. Respondents thought 'foreigners' no longer look up to us (20–30 years ago 65 per cent said they did, only 10 per cent are of that opinion now) and that 'we' no longer show people in other countries how they should do things (70 per cent thought we lead the world 20–30 years ago, only 23 per cent feel that still holds true). When asked how much confidence they had in the monarchy as an institution only 12 per cent said they had a 'great deal' of confidence in the monarchy, 23 per cent said 'quite a lot', 42 per cent said 'not very much' and 23 per cent 'none at all'. There were no comparative figures for previous years, the question had not been asked.

Why do we still have a monarchy? Because our clapped out constitution keeps us in matching red, white and blue dresses with puffy sleeves, in other words, in our infancy. We may increasingly know that these clothes don't quite fit any more, that they are outdated, but we're frightened to redesign the wardrobe. None of my peers really believe there will ever be a republic in this country, they think the monarchy is too deeply embedded in our culture. Maybe we'll end up with a Scandinavian type arrangement, they say. Diamond thinks that the time is not yet ripe for the referendum Charter 88 proposes: 'People aren't ready. It's now "okay" to question the monarchy, but there isn't yet a widespread, rational debate about the constitutional issues.'

My feeling is this: that we can and ought to make common cause with our parents, building on shared concerns about an overweening executive and an infinitely corruptible system of government. We will have to convince them that our monarchical constitution is holding their children back, that it is stifling our initiative. Above all we have to convince them that there is something stronger and more vital to replace it. This is a challenge, for us as much as for them. Citizenship is not purely about being well-governed, important though that is, it is about accepting our individual and collective responsibility for keeping democracy alive and kicking rather than shuffling it off onto someone else, elected or otherwise. A republic that did not embody this principle would be just as empty a shell as a monarchy.

HILARY WAINWRIGHT

ACROSS TO LONDON

WHEN I WAS a child in Leeds, the adults around me always spoke of going 'up to London'. This was sometimes associated with a mysterious promise of going 'up to London to see the Queen' or at least, the changing of her guards.

There is a danger in discussing republicanism within the framework of a debate about the monarchy. The danger is that we continue to look upwards. We define our republic in terms of the kind of head of state we want and the means by which we choose them. We end up simply secularising oligarchic power.

Tom Nairn has described how in Britain's unwritten constitution, monarchical government sanctifies centralised power. The monarchy gives the state 'a controlling interest in popular national identity – to the point that "state" and society have gone on seeming as one, and most of society's instincts can still be channeled upwards into adoration of the Crown'.

On this understanding of the role of the monarchy, democratic republicanism must be about more than changing the head of state. It must be about citizens participating on an equal basis in the control of public affairs. The abolition of the monarchy is therefore a necessary but not sufficient condition for a republic.

The abolition or emasculation of the monarchy, would only create an opportunity for democratic republicanism. It would not mark its achievement. It would break the lynchpin which at present binds together the centralised powers of Westminster, Whitehall and the City. To grasp the opportunity offered by a self-destructive Royal Family and a consequent weakening – no doubt temporary – of the monarchy, before the secular oligarchs establish new means of maintaining their power, republicans need to direct their attention to ways of mobilising the power for popular self-government. We need to start by clarifying the principles of self-government. The best place to start is with a visionary statement by Tom Paine.

In his argument for representative government against monarchy, Paine made the following statement: 'It appears to general observation, that revolutions create genius and talents; but those events do no more than bring them forward. There is existing in man, a mass of sense lying in a dormant state, and which unless something excites to action, will descend with him, in that condition, to the grave. As it is to the advantage of society that the whole of its faculties should be employed, the construction of government ought to be such as to bring forward by quiet and regular operation, all that extent of capacity which never fails to appear in revolution.'

In other words, in Paine's vision of a republic claims for political equality were inseparable from the presumption of cultural equality and hence the popular capacity for self-government. A fundamental criterion for democratic institutions would, on this basis, be whether or not they enable people's knowledge, practical as well as theoretical, to be developed and utilised for public benefit.

In the evolution of representative democracy in Britain, these two components of the radical republican tradition have become separated. The goal of cultural revolution has been marginalised. Reformers from the English middle and upper classes, unchallenged by deferential leaders of labour, have found it easier to campaign for political and even economic equality than to shed cultural attitudes of superiority. Beatrice Webb expressed the sentiment behind this powerful obstacle to self-government when she said, in her famous diary: 'The average sensual man can describe his problem but is unable to prescribe a solution'. This paternalistic resistance to cultural revolution has meant that the labour movement has rarely imagined, let alone practised, political arrangements distinct from those of the British state. And yet it is at the base of the labour movement that the popular impetus to self-government is frequently to be found.

There have been powerful movements of popular protest, at times leading to sustained economic self-organisation: the experiences of the early shop stewards and tenants movements; the Women's Co-operative Guild; the trades councils and other local sections of the labour movement from the General Strike right through to the recent organisation of women in the mining communities all provide evidence for this. The continuing paternalism of Labour and Liberal leaders – leaders of the two parties which in different ways claim to represent the democratic traditions of the French Revolution – has meant that these periodic awakenings of the desire for self-government have rarely led to the constitutional change by which this desire could become the basis of lasting institutions (or even proposals for such changes).

The experiment of the Greater London Council between 1982 and its abolition in 1986 has been the most extended recent attempt to uproot the foundations of paternalism from a public institution in Britain. Central to the new structures which the GLC was in the process of creating were formal mechanisms for sharing power between the GLC, an institution of representative democracy, and democratic popular organisations in the locality and the workplace.

Consider, for example, the GLC's policy of supporting inner London communities against the pressures of City property speculation. The GLC's strategy was to work in partnership with representative local groups. This included entrusting these organisations, when the GLC had taken over threatened land, with the development of the local area. Democratic local organisations carried out their own form of development within guidelines negotiated with the GLC and backed by its finance and expertise. In the process, formal institutional arrangements were established to frame the power – setting conditions and limits – of democratic non-state organisations in the making and implementing of policy.

The GLC experience and other attempts to enable

democratic civic organisations to play a formal part in government – while preserving their autonomy and popular roots – point to an essential but under-recognised dimension of constitutional reform. They provide the dimension required by Paine's notion that 'the construction of government ought to be such as to bring forward by quiet and regular operation, all that extent of capacity.'

The well established agenda of constitutional reform includes one set of changes designed to protect individuals from the state and a second dealing with the representation of the people in formulating the will of the state. I would like to bring to the fore a third and necessary component, giving constitutional form to cultural equality: these changes concern the institutions necessary to enable people to participate in the government of all public affairs, administrative as well as legislative.

This programme of constitutional reform must start at the base of society, with the ways in which people are already striving for democratic self-government. It must work upwards from an understanding of the voluntary associations which people already create to govern some of their affairs. It will have to address how and on what conditions these can be given wider public support, the level at which these associations should have sovereignty or joint sovereignty and the level at which wider and 'higher' decision making bodies are required. Only on the basis of the differentiated but integrated mechanisms of self-government which would emerge from such a process, could one assess the role and character of a head of state. What will there be left for them to do? There will be something, no doubt. But reversing Tom Nairn's observations about our present political arrangements, society's instincts would have been channelled towards reciprocal relations within different parts and different levels. We will no longer talk of going 'up to London' but – when we talk about it at all – 'across to London'.

TOM NAIRN

A STORY'S END

The two greatest Concernments that God hath in the world, the one is that of Religion. . .The other thing cared for is the Civil Liberty and Interest of the Nation – which I think is the next best God hath given men in this world.

Cromwell, Letters & Speeches (1904 ed)

WE ARE ONLY debating the future of the monarchy because it has none. 'Modernisation' – the chorus of the salvationists – already means something uncomfortably close to resurrection. The modernisers resemble those who used to throng the death-chamber of an absolute monarch moaning, even after the last breath: 'He hasn't really gone!'; 'God will not let him leave us!'; 'Morto, Lui. . . ma non e possibile!', and so on.

What is it that has died? Not the sovereign or the institution, but the enchantment – a near-universal romance with the Crown, coloured by adulation and protected by a strong emotional taboo. The end came incredibly quickly. It was as if the nation had been totally absorbed in the same romantic novel for about a hundred years, oblivious to all distractions and stern remarks about low-brow taste. Suddenly (round about the time of the Windsor Castle fire) it appears to have reached the end of the tale. Sighing deeply, it rubbed its eyes as if waking up, and threw the book away.

The book – the real story, the all-encompassing text at the back of the national mind – has been discarded. It is now some years since Benedict Anderson pointed out that nations are really books. In *Imagined Communities* he argued that print

151

technology was a necessary condition of nationalism. The presence of the state in the individual cranium would not be possible without it. Authority can only be refracted downwards and outwards on an accessible vehicle. Since accessibility is defined by language – or idiom, vernacular style – national particularity assumed a new salience in world politics. The vehicles of imagined community became those of development namely modernisation and the forced progress towards industrialism.

Industrialisation therefore requires walking books, or national stories. Nationalism is 'not simply invented', a mere fictive notion. Real socio-economic development has – so far – needed such inventions in order to be carried forward. Imagined communities cannot beget real ones; however, real (or potential) communities do appear to require an imagined version of themselves to function within modernity. Also, potential societies can become real by employing the leverage which imagination supplies.

Now let's read the argument in reverse. What happens when a country loses its book? When the story has actually ended, can there be a further narrative? At bedtime tomorrow night no-one is going to resume the old story, or invent a new chapter for it. Of course,the characters and incidents are all still there, and in one sense the tale could easily be carried on. But if it has become boring – if the listener no longer enters into the spirit – then there is no point in continuing.

Were this just one national book amongst others, the situation might not be so critical. But it is not! As a long-standing opponent of monarchy, I have made as many mistakes about it as anybody else. But one at least I hope I have avoided: underestimating its importance. The monarchy was a great story. For several generations it literally bestrode a world half in love with it.

It was a story which worked, in the basic sense of Anderson's theory. It carried Great Britain forward, and resulted in a strange pact with industrialisation. The natural progenitor of so much that is modern kept its own distance from modernity: the identity-story which enabled this clung to the patrician and to hierarchy, confining industrial development within boundaries that were at once regional and social. Imperial over-expansion limited industry and technology, rather than giving them their reckless head.

Naturally, critics always saw the downside of all this. But until the 1950s it produced a working accommodation that suited England's heartland. And the Royal Story made it into an effective popular fable – a sense of 'who we are' and of our communal and reasonably exalted place in the world. It was a structure which lasted from 1760–1990, approximately. Historians like Linda Colley and David Cannadine have traced its origins in the eighteenth century, and we have all experienced its collapse.

The same writers have shown how the monarchy was a 'stretched' identity, English at the core yet extended through many annexes to match the multi-national nature of the British Isles and its foreign possessions. There was always the risk that 'extension' might mean 'dilution' But it was this very risk which encouraged the astonishing build-up of royalist hype from Queen Victoria onwards – as if only exaggerated romance could keep the thing going. The functional passion of Britain's imagined community had a driving purpose, therefore – not for nothing were people so emotional about the monarchy for so long. It was not exactly Britain's nationalism, more a unique *sui generis* substitute for it: a story covering much of the same ground, expressing many of the relevant feelings, and providing a strong expression of identity free from ethnic risks. The over-heated romance of The Crown did provide a pseudo-ethnic closeness. All nationalism prescribes an extended family, a simulacrum of blood-ties. But the Anglo-British had an actual family to appropriate those ethnic impulses. The Royal Family was the symbolic ethos of a state structurally at risk from genuine ethnicity.

Now abruptly, the story seems to have abruptly deconstructed itself. In the world of literary criticism deconstruction is a subtle scholarly performance where the object falls apart metaphorically, revealing the omnipotent sapience of its conceptual dissector. Reality, however, merely falls apart. The bits take over, devoid of their original sense, but propelled onward, at least for a time. The centre has not held and cluelessness is abroad. Nobody has any notion of what to do next.

When trouble is so deep, superficial therapies appeal. One example is the formula of modernisation of the Windsors. Another derives from Europe – the hope that Britain is already aboard another vehicle that will take it forward. A new and ready-made identity comes with this ticket, saving one from horrid navel-searching and nastiness. A few adjustments to the royals, a few more to the Europeanized UK, and all will be if not exactly well, tolerable.

Charter 88's closet republicanism is of course a profounder recipe than any of these. Envisaging a modernised and new state, it goes far beyond recommending a few adjustments. It appeals for a revolution by consent, in which a new politics takes over from the old and the Crown vanishes amid the excitement. The Charter suggests there is no longer any need to be overtly republican. By the time the new story is in place, it will simply feel absurd to include royalty in it. New stories generate their own characters. A president will appear inevitable. The same people who nowadays cannot imagine a presidency will discover that they want to vote for the equivalents of a Mary Robinson, a Pertini or a Von Weiszacker.

I like the argument, but I don't quite believe it. This may have something to do with my coming from Scotland, and being a student of nationalism. What bothers anyone from an ethnic periphery is an uneasy sense that there will be other things in the final story. 'Identity' is about entrails, as well as aspirations. Amongst other things the Windsor monarchy has been a glorious conjuring-trick for sublimating the entrails of Englishness. Over-identification with the monarchy carried England into an odd neglect of the native self. Neglect can be a form of repression and repression breeds its own return. A nation defined at one end by the Royal Household has the Chelsea Casuals and Essex Man at the other. Ask any representatives of Black Britain as they know all about the latter, and are unrepresented in the former.

Our suspicion is fortified by two other considerations. One is rather general, and theoretical. Constitutions do not exist in a stratosphere called Civilization where pure blueprints of legitimacy can be drafted, imposed, and mean the same wherever they happen to function. However much it shares with other, comparable systems a constitution also forms an amalgam with its society. It cannot escape marriage with a national identity. Secondly, the actual way that the old national story came to an end has an effect. The fable was destroyed by Thatcherism, not by reason.

What will take its place? In one sense nothing can. It is an irreparable falling out of love. But in another sense something almost certainly will. The monarchy-modernisers are not wrong to see that some continuation or substitute will be needed, though I doubt that a taxed, tidied-up and ordinarified Crown answers the need. Any reply to this question depends partly on how one views the Royal past. Why were the readers of this tale so absorbed, and for so long? Why were their emotions so engaged? What did the fable do for them?

I believe that this symbolic apparatus helped to define a national identity. Not alone, of course. There were and still are other social and cultural building blocks involved, some of them more important: Westminster and the non-written constitution, for instance, or the palaeontology of British 'class'. However, the monarchy was essential to the formation of the coherent structure – an 'identity' or 'imagined community' – demanded by a nation-state.

It worked. A popular addiction was formed, and the preposterous myth of sovereignty was retained as the keystone of Westminster constitutionalism. That it functioned so well is all the more surprising when one looks back to the ethnic-English identity which preceded Britishness. During the monarchy's recent decline and fall, 'Englishness' has become a novel object of puzzlement and cultural surmise. I recommend all those amazed by its discovery to turn immediately to Liah Greenfeld's account of the real Old Adam in her brilliant comparative study, *Nationalism: Five Roads to Modernity* (Harvard University Press, 1992). She points out that English nationalism was the original patent later taken up, mostly without acknowledgement, by the rest of the world. The patent has been around so long that the inventors have forgotten it. The monarchy was one of the ways of forgetting. Now it's gone, I expect the older story will come back to them.

PATRICK WRIGHT

PALACES OF THE MIND

IT DID OCCUR to me during the course of the Queen's 'annus horribilis' that the House of Windsor had become almost uninhabitable, that it had got to the point where nobody could breathe the air, and maybe that what we needed was a new charity without royal sponsorship which was made up, perhaps, of a privatised arm of the security services that would rescue these people, give them false identities, and rehouse them in the suburbs. The problem that I have with the kind of sneering that has been going on, the reason that when I talk with Richard Littlejohn I find myself still at a polite distance from much of his argument in this area, is that the House of Windsor has been built smack in the middle of the national imagination, and therefore when we start talking about what happens to it, or smirking and laughing at it, we in a sense are talking about ourselves very intimately.

Here are a couple of cameos which raise the question of how royalty got to be so established in the national mind. I will limit myself to two individuals, two members of the Windsor family, both of whom have achieved a reputation for talking to plants, although that is not entirely the purpose of my choice.

The first is George III. Things happened to him in Weymouth, where he went seriously mad. In June 1789 he had a small retinue and three coaches, which left Windsor and set off for Weymouth to take curative water and to do sea-bathing and those other things which were then novel. It is quite interesting to follow that route down because the pamphleteers are sitting there talking as he gets to one part of the

157

New Forest and he is awarded a brace of white greyhounds by the mayor; there were crowds cheering and waving at everybody, and some of the pamphleteers start writing from the viewpoint of the white greyhounds, for example. They get to Salisbury, and they travel through some hastily erected triumphal arches and one of the pamphleteers wonders whether it is really appropriate to be passing through triumphal arches at this point in George's career. He lists a number of reasons for gloom: they include the fact that the trouble-making radical John Wilkes had not been imprisoned for life, that the House of Commons was full of obnoxious members who could not be expelled, that the press had not been brought under full ministerial control, that America had not been conquered and brought to constitutional obedience, that the liberties of the Dutch had not been completely dislodged, and as for the French Revolution nobody even wished to talk about it. Of course, the other factor that made everybody very interested in this journey was that apparently in Windsor Park in his madness George III had been seen talking to an oak tree.

So there we are, with a fairly crestfallen and difficult monarch, a man in a bad position, travelling down to this remote town of Weymouth. He can't go to any more established resort like Brighton because his son is behaving so appallingly badly there. Indeed his son's friends are so degenerate and immoral that one in particular, a man called Lord Broudenall, was known as 'Cockie' by the general public rather than 'Your Honour'. Here is King George going pointedly in the other direction. What is intriguing about the result is that when he gets to Weymouth, he is turned into something that is called a 'patriot king'. This is a phrase that had been used in the 1730s to define one of the possibilities open to the monarchy, but George III was the man who really pulled this off.

What this consisted of was partly a cult of visibility. George was down there and he had his private rooms, but he would eat his meals in public, he would walk up and down the esplanade, and even when he wanted to do things in private, he would allow the public in to look at him, so that there would be big meals in which there would be an audience that was allowed into the rooms they were eating in to sit and watch for ten minutes and then they would be told to go and the meal would continue. He even bathed in public; the British Library has copies of designs for a special kind of barge that would enable the monarch to bathe without anybody seeing, but the choice was made that the whole event should take place in public from ordinary bathing machines with a band playing 'God Save the King', a relatively recent tune at that time.

Some interesting anonymous novels came out about this particular summer and they defined the patriot king in a fairly unusual way. I will run through some of these characteristics. First of all, he was not an expansionist enlarging the boundaries of his dominions (in other words we had lost America) but instead the wise governor, the man of justice who supports agriculture and keeps a truly paternal eye on the liberties, morals, and well-being of his people. Secondly, he was against excess, knowing that the tide of luxury can be more destructive to national welfare than ever the sword can be. Thirdly, his address was not only to the aristocracy and court, 'not the splendours of court or the pomp of crowded levees, but the real distinction is to go to the middle and lower orders of society, to let them contemplate and admire the bright assemblage of every moral perfection which beams conspicuously in the Royal Family'. He was a constitutionalist and there is talk about 'an enviable constitution guarded by the auspices of the patriot king'. He was an improver who, unlike Alexander the Great and numerous other foreign historical rulers, was not great without improving the lives of the people. He was 'a man of fortitude, he was firm in the purpose of public good, and had sufficient greatness of mind to enable him to despise the arrows of calumny'. He was 'a man of ripe reason' (a pointed remark, I guess) 'and sound policy, and a man of moderation and private virtue'.

So you basically have a re-establishment of the monarch around a set of patriotic virtues that were quite new. Looking into this in her book *Britons*, Linda Colley expands on exactly this side of what George III was up to. People in Weymouth would stand there (these books are full of them) and they would commend the fact that George had discarded the splendour of royalty while still preserving sovereignty in the hearts of the people. One female invalid in a novel called *Cousin Sarah* remarked after seeing George III that 'royalty does you more good than all the drugs in the world.'

As Linda Colley says about this period, a new compact is made between the monarch and the people. It is entirely an imaginative compact, it is an act that creates a sense of nationhood. This is the primary symbol of Britishness as it was defined at that crucial moment. It included the use of art, for example, the portraits that were distributed to embassies, the founding of the Royal Academy of Arts, royal reporting which was controlled in the press and filtered from the national press down through local newspapers; it included a linkage of royal celebration with public works – the business of the Queen with the trowel has its origins at this time – so that where there is a royal pageant there is usually a civic improvement of some sort or another. There is a strong address to schoolchildren. One of Linda Colley's most interesting points is that at this point there is a particular address towards women. For example, George III's first Jubilee came up when a middle-class woman from the Welsh borders suggested that it might be a good idea to have proper celebrations.

As Colley points out – the alternative to this role was woman as the constant provider of sexual scandal. This was the destabilising role that women played in the life of the court, and the other was as the provider of 'sentimental female attachment'. So you can see all of this being put together, this form of imaginative theatre if you like, in the shadow of the French Revolution, in the shadow of the winning of American independence.

By the time we get to the 1980s, we find my second botanist, who is Prince Charles. After the Second World War the circumstances which enabled that particular form of patriotism to be sustained in the eighteenth century and into the nineteenth century have gone. We are dealing with a royal family that is having to be pretty ingenious about where it goes to find or to remake the patriotic bond. Thinking schematically about this, it is interesting that the Queen establishes some bond with the level of family life in one way or another. The attachments that the monarchy forms can be interestingly errant as well. Take the Queen Mother. It struck me in the 80s that while Margaret Thatcher was rising she had plenty of use for the mythology of the Second World War: she had lots to say about the Battle of Britain, the spirit of Dunkirk, the terrible defeat and the heroic fight-back. She didn't have anything to say about the Blitz, which was one of the most pre-eminent bits of mythology of them all, about people pulling together; it was a sort of sentimental pastoral dream, if you like, that out of this heat and torment we will create a new Britain called the Welfare State.

In the eighties all that was left to the Queen Mum: she was there to do her re-visits to the East End. It was not on Mrs Thatcher's political agenda. Prince Charles, before his fall from grace into the set of marital problems that he is now embroiled in, seemed to me to be highly interesting in the sense that here he was, constrained by protocol, trying to find serious issues. For ten or fifteen years he went through what is known as the periphery of national life – after all he can't be dealing with politics, protocol demands he go to the edges – and what he comes up with is a most extraordinary collection of themes. Organic farming, local distinctiveness, architecture, homeopathy, plain speech, grammer, craft, ornamentation, the threatened varieties of English apple (he funds the station that keeps them alive), pollution; we've got a prince of local variety, he's a sort of Gerald Manley Hopkins prince: he likes dappled things and barns that lift the spirit; he's the prince of a traditional form of perception.

I look at this and I think it's amazing. At some level what we have got here is a man who has turned himself into the Prince of Eccentricities. But what is intriguing about the story is that, when you go to the edges of the society we've been living in for the last ten or twenty years, what you find is actually not very peripheral at all, in fact in a funny way you beat your way into the very centre of things. Because with a political culture of the centre that is not addressing numerous issues, and a roving monarch who knows he has got to keep away from the centre, one thing after another that he picks up turns out to be explosive. There he suddenly was in the inner city. There he was promoting that curious version of outward bound that is called business sponsorship. He was there at all these points where the energies, forms, aspirations of the culture that weren't addressed in the centre were living. I thought that what he did in the eighties, despite his own intention, was to produce a kind of bizarre royalist demonstration of how the periphery and the centre are fundamentally connected – that what may look like eccentricity is actually what's been pushed to the edges.

Where do we go with this? What I conclude is that there's no question that the Royal Family lives by the compact that it is able to make with the national imagination. The problem perhaps comes up when we turn that question around and say does the national imagination live by the compacts that royalty makes with it or that it makes with royalty? One cannot be so sure at all.

These themes which Charles has addressed have been picked up and made eccentric by his involvement – this was certainly the case with his concern with architecture. Architecture was a strongly central theme in the eighties for a good reason. It was a place where people could address the public interest when it was completely off the agenda of the main political parties, all of them, whether they were triumphant or frightened at that time. It was a place where people could talk about the sixties; they could talk about life in dreadful high-rise council developments, which the architectural profession had given up on by 1968 but which people are still living in. Charles was returning to a lot of questions that needed to be opened in certain senses, but the difficulty is that once Charles gets on to these things they all tend to go terribly wrong. So you end up with a ghastly polarisation in architecture – a ludicrous situation where serious houses for the new rich are being offered as a symbolic answer for the failings of public housing in Brent or Liverpool. It could not get more absurd than this.

Take organic farming which, if you stop to think about it, has just about got beyond muck and mysticism and the murky blood-and-soil attachments which it had in the thirties and is beginning to talk about how we deal with less intensive agriculture. At that very point where the concept of set-aside can become something sensible in the landscape, when the government is beginning to put tiny amounts of money into schemes for less intensive, organic forms of agriculture, when the supermarkets are stocking this stuff, along comes Charles and we're back with a rather mad mystic vision of organicism of the most dubious kind. That's the issue about the monarchy which we've got to face.

The level of debate when issues are raised by the Royal Family seems to me to be dreadful. We get immediate polarisation, not reasoned debate. We get terrible unctuousness from courtiers and whippersnapper bite-back from critics who know that they can't get their heads chopped off any more. We don't get a form of discussion that takes the issue forward. We also get a kind of tight-lipped secrecy: in the architectural world I've talked to people whom I've known for years, and because they've had a certain dinner on a certain day they can't speak for months about anything. It's a crippling form of deference. It's not open, it's not constructive, and it's not helpful. During that period when Prince Charles seemed to be drumming up the agenda, when he seemed to be setting up to be the monarch of the welfare state ten years after everyone else had given up on the welfare state, we had all these very seriously interesting debates reduced to a series of monarchical interventions. So buildings didn't get built which should have been built, buildings which shouldn't have been built did get built. In the end that is perhaps the most insidious aspect of our situation: we are dealing with a monarchy that isn't working within a consistent, reasonable, democratic framework, but is actually parasitic on the public imagination and never more so than when it addresses really vital themes.

ANTHONY HOLDEN

WE WILL GO QUIETLY

> So long as the human heart is strong and the human reason
> weak, royalty will be strong because it appeals to diffused
> feeling, and republics weak because they appeal to the under-
> standing.
>
> Walter Bagehot, *The English Constitution*

KING FAROUK OF Egypt predicted that by the end of the
twentieth century there would be only five monarchs left in the
world: the Kings of England, hearts, diamonds, clubs and
spades. Maybe he spoke too soon. On 4 February 1993, at two
North London branches of William Hill, an unnamed middle-
aged Briton placed bets totalling £8,000 on the abolition of the
British monarchy by the year 2000. If history proves him right,
this canny punter stands to win £146,000. 'We don't know
who he is,' said William Hill, 'but he didn't have big ears, he
didn't have a posh voice, and he certainly didn't have a mobile
phone.' In the first two months of 1993, British bookies felt
obliged to shorten the odds against the monarchy's imminent
demise from 100–1 to 1–5.

'We will go quietly' has for years been a standard joke in the
Queen's social repertoire, which may yet return to haunt her.
'After all,' as her heir has said, 'if people don't want it, they
won't have it.' This simple truth, Prince Charles continued,
makes the monarchy 'a kind of elective institution' – a piece of
royal semantics which surely stretches contemporary notions
of democracy to the outer limits of optimism. His more

pragmatic father, Prince Philip, speaks less in riddles than in earnest: 'To survive, the monarchy must change.'

Will the eighth dynasty to have sat on the British throne in more than a thousand years turn out to be the last? As it flounders amid personal and financial controversy, facing calls for fundamental constitutional reform, the next foreseeable milestone is Elizabeth II's golden jubilee in 2002, when she will be seventy-five years old and her son Charles fifty-three. For the Royal House of Windsor to reach that anniversary intact, it must ensure that the monarchy is perceived as a relevant force for good in the modern world, rather than an antique, outmoded repository of hereditary wealth and privilege. As long as its tenants live in extravagant luxury at public expense, hoarding their huge private wealth – and failing, in some cases, to maintain the high moral standards which are the price of such privilege – the monarchy's chances of survival sink daily.

It would surely be wrong for the British throne to fall because of the short-comings, moral or otherwise, of its transient occupants. It should give way, with as much dignity as logic, to the will of a people anxious to better their future with more appropriate constitutional arrangements. But the longer it takes the Windsors to set their House in order, the more the Crown will be seen as an obstacle to – rather than a safeguard of – basic democratic freedoms. From the demise of the monarchy would flow a written constitution, an elected second chamber of parliament and the separation of church and state. These reforms would pave the way for a Bill of Rights, a Supreme Court, a Freedom of Information Act and all the other civic rights taken for granted in most modern democracies, but denied the British so long as they remain subjects rather than citizens. This constitutional renaissance would be *possible* under a radically reformed monarchy; but it would be *inevitable* if Britain were to become a European republic.

Given the longevity of all royal women in this century, not least the Queen's own mother, the present reign seems likely to last long enough for the British people to make a considered choice for their future. Either the royal family will use the time to ride out its current notoriety, perhaps even to embody the national way of life by finally beginning to share it, or a popular consensus will see its way through to greater realism and greater democracy: entrusting its sense of national dignity to an elected, accountable worthy, in office briefly enough to enhance it. Increasingly, at last, Britons are beginning to question the hereditary principle as an appropriate method in the twentieth century to choose their head of state. So much is done in his or her name, supposedly on their behalf, that they are asking whether they might not perhaps be entitled to some say in the choice of the individual purporting to represent their identity and aspirations.

At present, the politicians elected by the British people are pleased to call themselves Her Majesty's Government and Her Majesty's Loyal Opposition. The Queen's peace is kept by the Royal Navy and the Royal Air Force. It is illegal to mail a letter which does not bear the Queen's head, and inelegant not to speak the Queen's English. Even if separate parliaments are eventually won by the Scots and the Welsh, not to mention the embattled inhabitants of Northern Ireland, they and the English will all still cohabit a federal state called the United Kingdom.

Are the British ready to put their heads before their hearts – their understanding, in Bagehot's terms, before their feelings – and choose their head of state, by democratic means, from among their own number? Though self-evidently logical, it is a leap of faith which seems at odds with the national character. 'Monarchy is neither necessary nor sufficient to a democratic constitution', conceded *The Times* recently, reaching the less-than-inspiring conclusion that 'the strength of the British constitution lies as much in surviving the monarchy as in benefiting from it'.

This British gift for paradox – or is it, perhaps, self-punishment? – will surely remain the crown's best hope for survival. No matter how reasonable the arguments advanced in favour of an elected head of state – in favour, in other words, of that dread word 'republic' – the British still clap their hands to their ears, ever dreaming of pageantry and princesses. But it is not just the failure of several royal marriages, notably that of the heir to the throne, which has brought the monarchy to its current plight. Nor is it merely the abuse of their public trust by certain members of the Royal Family. It is the failure of the hereditary head of state and her advisers to mirror change in the institution which is supposed to symbolize national life. So long as the monarchy remains redolent of Britain's lost empire – and thus, in Dean Acheson's famous phrase, of her lost role –it will compound Britain's failure to face its future as a European nation-state. Neither crown nor government has yet acknowledged it, but this is the central flaw which has brought the monarchy so low: clinging to a sumptuous imperial past rather than shedding its *ermine* to face a more modest European future. John Major's supposedly egalitarian Britain is meanwhile expected to muddle through with an unelected head of state, and a Prime Minister elected with a narrow majority on a minority of votes whose 'big idea' is a Citizen's Charter for consumers who are not even citizens.

Unless government is prepared to haul a reluctant monarchy through its expensively-subsidized looking-glass, out of that Victorian world of imperial make-believe into the more straitened Britain of the twenty-first century, there is little hope for the House of Windsor – and, more importantly, there is less for Britain. All the portents of the monarchy's present troubles were apparent during the 1980s, the meritocratic 'Thatcher decade', long before the embarrassments of 1992 – the Queen's 'annus horribilis' which publicly shamed the Crown into minor cosmetic change. During the Thatcher years, for all the Prime Minister's fierce personal loyalty to the Crown, the institution of monarchy was already beginning to look dangerously out of synch with the times. By the end of Thatcher's first decade in power, Royal House of Windsor Ltd was at least as bloated and inefficient as any of the nationalized industries she had so ruthlessly privatized. In October 1990 the Institute of Economic Affairs (IEA), an influential, free-market group renowned as Thatcher's favourite think tank, issued a policy document calling for the sovereign to be stripped of her remaining constitutional duties and reduced to a merely symbolic role in British life. Power should be transferred, it argued, to 'an officer appointed by parliament'. As long as the monarchy held popular appeal, it would be worth retaining only as 'an emblem of historical continuity in British life' and 'an alternative focus for popular attention away from political leaders.'

With a cynicism worthy of Bagehot, in other words, the IEA was suggesting that the monarchy be reduced to a mere tourist attraction, its constitutional value as a smokescreen to provide the British voter with a sense of well-being while the politicians did their worst. The document's appearance was timed to coincide with early drafts of the Conservative party's manifesto for the forthcoming general election, which at that time offered every prospect of a 'hung' parliament. The monarch's prime constitutional function – the selection of a senior politician to form a government – becomes 'difficult', it argued, when no party has an overall majority. 'At that moment the Crown is politicized and alternative, transparent, non-monarchical procedures become important. In so far as the Crown has a wider constitutional significance, it is a negative one – the confusion of the status of the citizen with the status of the subject.'

The IEA document also recommended a written constitution (to 'buttress' the United Kingdom against the rest of the European community), and an elected second chamber of parliament, from which hereditary peers would be excluded. Two years earlier, Thatcher had said that her government owed a great debt to the 'leadership' of the IEA; that June, however, she had warned European leaders at the Dublin summit against any moves that might have constitutional implications for 'our beloved Queen'. So which way would the lady turn? The question proved academic. Within a month the document had suddenly been withdrawn, without explanation, and Thatcher had in any case lost office, giving way to a successor more tempted by fine-tuning than wholescale upheaval. On paper, the Queen could breathe again. But an uncomfortable atmosphere prevailed, in which the forces of left and right seemed to be forming an unholy alliance against the Crown.

Another of Thatcher's legacies, symbolized by the Murdoch press and its tabloid brethren, was a diminution of deference among the 'lower' orders to their betters, the monarchy foremost among them. As Disraeli wrote to Matthew Arnold: 'Everyone likes flattery; and when it comes to royalty, you should lay it on with a trowel.' Typical of the prevailing servility among parliamentarians was the remark of Edward Heath, the former Conservative Prime Minister, that the demise of the Wales marriage was 'one of the saddest announcements made by a prime minister in modern times'. Sadder than Black Wednesday? Or Bloody Sunday? Or the deaths of 255 British troops in the Falklands conflict? Heath's fawning was reminiscent of the reveries of the Archbishop of Canterbury after Elizabeth II's coronation: 'Last Tuesday this country and Commonwealth were not far from the kingdom of heaven.' Or of the day in 1977, when the Queen went to Westminster Hall on the occasional of her silver jubilee, to receive a 'loyal address' from both houses of parliament: a velvet curtain had been discreetly drawn across the plaque recording that it was here that King Charles I was sentenced to death.

But the generation of Britons now advancing toward the seats of power no longer shares its parents' unthinking, tribal deference toward the Crown. In the words of the Conservative MP George Walden: 'Anyone in authority who does not understand that huge swathes of the country, mostly those under forty and by no means on the left, have had it up to here with royalty, is putting the future of the monarchy at risk. . .What sort of country do we want? Reproduction antique?'

Walden's leader, John Major, sees the monarchy as 'a very precious part of our way of life – a rock of stability in a changing world'. But he also thinks that the Queen's offer to pay a modest degree of income tax has 'brought the monarchy up to date'. To Major, that one concession is enough to make it 'an institution relevant to the 1990s, just as a hundred years ago it was an institution relevant to the 1890s. . . The monarchy has evolved and changed. I think the Queen has judged it very well.'

The current atmosphere suggests otherwise: that the monarchy will have to 'change and evolve' rather more to ensure even its medium-term survival. As Roy Hattersley has warned: 'The Establishment always responds to the threat of real reform by making some concessions to the reformers.' On the financial front alone, little has happened to outdate the view expressed by the early feminist Vera Brittain, the mother of Baroness (Shirley) Williams, that the Royals are "expensive lunatics kept in motors and stables by an industrious nation's toil" '.

In a better Britain, with a reformed constitution, it might be possible to wish the Prince of Wales well in any second marriage he might care to make – which would no more prevent him becoming king than environment secretary, president of the Royal Institute of British Architects or manager of the England polo team. The only difference is that the first job would be his by virtue of hereditary, while the rest would require some evidence of ability, in competition with other candidates. As it stands, defending our constitution demands hypocrisy as breathtaking as that of the legal adviser to the General Synod of the Church of England, who has baldly declared that there is 'nothing in statute law to say that a monarch can't be divorced and Supreme Governor' – thus sweeping aside most canon law to preserve the Church's handy alliance with the Crown.

If either church, crown or indeed government wishes the monarchy to reflect a modern Britain, the first step would be to repeal two eighteenth-century statutes: the 1772 Royal Marriages Act, which forbids the heir to the throne to marry outside the Protestant faith; and the 1701 Act of Settlement, which ordains that any royal who 'shall profess the popish religion or shall marry a papist' must be treated 'as if said person were naturally dead'. Both are clearly offensive in today's multi-ethnic, multi-racial Britain – especially at a time of schism in the established church, when 'the greatest upheaval since the Reformation' is driving increasing numbers of both clergy and laity to take their faith elsewhere. Although the Act of Settlement's repeal would endanger the House of

Windsor's legal claim to the throne, even as staunch a royalist as Lady Longford wishes to be rid of it. Lord Tebbit's complaint that it would 'signal the end of the British monarchy by bringing it under the reach of Rome' she rightly dismisses as 'out of touch with the Europe of the future'.

The Europe of the future, whether federal or not, holds different challenges for the monarchy. The Queen may not share her subjects' concern about the potential loss of national sovereignty ('her family,' a courtier told Anthony Sampson, had 'long ago come to terms with losing their own political power'); but she should perhaps concern herself with other aspects of the Treaty of Maastricht. Professor David Cannadine, for one, finds it 'difficult to envisage a serious role for the British royal house in any tighter form of continental federation'.

To take Cannadine's point, it is not necessary to rouse the familiar apoplexy of such diehards as Lord (Woodrow) Wyatt by joining the 'lacklustre defeatists who see Britain ever dwindling in importance, a cipher on the world stage'. Nor is it just to read the Treaty, wherein it appears that the British monarch will henceforth join her subjects as a pliant citizen of Europe. It is to acknowledge that integration into 'the very heart of Europe' – the course on which John Major is determined to lead his 'classless' Britain, even against its will – may well involve constitutional arrangements more in line with those of our new democratic partners. If Britons are to be citizens of Europe, for instance, might it not be time for them to become citizens of Britain?

Where else in Europe is the citizenry part-governed by people who inherit their seats in parliament, unaccountable to any electorate? As Britain adapts to the European way of democracy, a stream of new and revised legislation should at last prove the need for a written constitution for this country, complete with a Bill of Rights. Were it to include provision for a Supreme Court, it might be possible to pursue civil and human rights cases without resort to the European Court at The Hague. Were it to lead to a Freedom of Information Act, the British disease of secrecy might join that of class on the list of threatened, if not yet endangered species.

Have Major's protracted negotiations ensured that his monarch will receive immunity from European employment and discrimination laws, as she does from her own? Has he seen to it that no European court will be able to summon her as a witness, even a defendant, as is the case in her own British courts? Will our European partners be content for the British sovereign to travel without a passport, drive without taking a test, own numerous dogs without buying a licence?

Which European monarch's face will appear on the integrated European currency, the federal European stamp? Rampant standardization throughout the community seems certain to force the British royal family to adapt to the ways of the 'bicycle kings' of Europe. Nothing could seem more likely to secure their future – unless, of course, they expect the taxpayer to pay for the bicycles. If the twenty-first century sees King William V performing the State Opening of Parliament in a suit and tie, rather than a crown and ermine robes, then the British monarchy will have been saved by the Maastricht Treaty. If His Majesty arrives in a Rolls-Royce rather than a golden horse-drawn coach, refers to himself in the singular rather than the plural, and does not expect elderly aristocrats to walk backwards before him, bearing 500-year-old relics on velvet cushions, Britain will at last have emerged from the long shadows of its past and woken up to its future. Maybe then it will find the maturity to let go of its nanny and elect a more representative head of state.

GEOFFREY ROBERTSON QC

A Silk's Eye View

ONE OF THE more arcane duties of a Queen's Counsel is to advise the monarch, when called upon, free of charge. This may be a *quid pro quo* for the royal monopoly which allows us to charge excessive fees to the common people. Let me emphasise at the outset that I have not been asked, as yet, to counsel Her Majesty. Nor have I made a fortune by regaling her with gratuitous advice in public print.

My concern for the future of the House of Windsor is really a concern for the future governance of Britain. What I have to suggest is that the laws which define and protect the monarchy are both obsolete and obnoxious, and that the only sensible way forward is to replace them with a modern Act of Settlement which allocates to the Crown a minimal, defined and secular role under a written constitution. Unless this can be accomplished during the reign of Charles III, I fear he may be the last of his line.

The laws which define the monarchy today embody the social and political attitudes of the bygone and barbaric ages when they were passed. None more so than the 1361 Treason Act, which still punishes with death any party to adultery with the wife of the monarch's eldest son and heir, whether she is separated from him or not. This monstrous legislation, still on the statute books, threatens the Princess of Wales with the fate of Anne Boleyn, should she aid and abet treason by surrendering willingly to the advances of anyone more common than herself.

Parliament has once reformed this law – in 1814. It replaced the executioner's block with the gallows as the preferred method of execution. I am happy to report, however, that should the Princess ever be convicted of the crime of treasonable adultery, she has the right to petition the Queen for one of the privileges which our unwritten constitution reserves for those of noble blood. She can ask to be beheaded rather than hanged by the neck until she is dead.

I imagine that the sale of television rights to the Princess of Wales' execution would pay the royal taxes for many years to come. But I do not detect any activity from Scotland Yard's Treason Squad, despite all the innuendo being peddlled by the tabloids. Anyway, in the unlikely event that an Old Bailey jury were even to convict the Princess of treason, a fairy tale Euro-ending would follow, since the Court of Human Rights in Strasbourg would find death a disproportionate penalty for making love, and the Queen would be required to grant a last-minute reprieve. The Princess could then serve out her commuted sentence in the Tower of London, along with her alternative court and her alternative courtiers, thereby serving that ultimately redeeming purpose of the Royal Family, to be an attraction for tourists.

Let us move on from 1361 to rather more modern legislation defining the monarchy, namely the Act of Settlement of 1700 which determines upon whom the Crown shall descend. On Protestants only, for a start. The Act provides that any monarch who holds communion with the Church of Rome, or who marries a papist – heaven forbid a Hindu or Muslim or Rastafarian – is immediately unthroned. His or her subjects are absolved by force of law from all their love and allegiance. This odious legislation enshrines religious intolerance in the very bedrock of the British constitution. Why would Charles be unfit to be king if he became a Methodist, or were to join the Lord Chancellor in the 'Wee Free'? As the law now stands, if Diana, while still married to Charles, took communion with priests from Rome, she could disinherit her children by the simple ploy of having them received into the Catholic Church during an access weekend. If this isn't objectionable enough, consider the rules of royal succession. These are based on the feudal principle of primogeniture, and inheritance by the males of the line, in blatant contravention of the Sex Discrimination Act. If Charles were unable or unwilling to ascend, why should the Crown fall upon the head of his infant male children, followed by Andrew and Edward, ahead of Anne, – perhaps the most deservedly popular of them all?

It is wholly unacceptable to have this sexist nonsense embodied in the rules for choosing a head of state. There are many more examples. The right to marry and found a family, guaranteed by Article 12 of the European Conventions is violated by the Royal Marriages Act of 1772. According to this legislation, still on our statute books, no descendant of George II under the age of 25 is permitted to marry without the sovereign's consent. And at no age can they marry without twelve months' notice to the Privy Council and the possibility of the wedding being scuppered by a joint resolution of both houses of Parliament.

As recently as 1976, an over-loyal Labour Home Secretary, (Mr Roy Jenkins), took care to ensure that the Race Relations Act would not apply to the Royal Household. That may explain why there are so few black faces amongst the royal courtiers even today, when parts of the black Commonwealth look like remaining by the turn of the century, the only independent nations still reigned over by the House of Windsor.

These laws which define and protect the Royal Family – against their wishes I hope – breach at least four articles of the European Convention on Human Rights. They are obsolete and obnoxious parts of our constitution.

There are many other laws relating to the Royal Family, most of which are merely silly (although the monarch's immunity from any legal action may not be amusing if you are run over by a royal motorcade): I do not really object to the law which vests property in every wild white swan in the realm in the Queen, nor to the fact that every whale, sturgeon or grampus landed in the kingdom belongs to her. Actually, the law states that the heads of what it terms 'the royal fish' should belong to the King and their tails to the Queen. On vital matters like these, our constitution is very explicit.

It is much less clear about trifling details such as which party gets to form the government in a hung parliament. But there you go. If you don't write down your rules, they will be invented or manipulated by those in power at the time. When the Prime Minister declares that the royal separation has no constitutional implications, that is only true because we have an Alice in Wonderland constitution which means what the Prime Minister wants it to mean.

Instead of a written constitution, we have a patchwork quilt of ancient and idiotic laws, supplemented by the conventions and traditions made up as we merrily and royally roll along. As a result we have no truly independent head of state. The monarch now accepts the advice – that's a euphemism for obeying the directions – of the government of the day. We lack an elected and respected figurehead, whose wisdom and integrity can provide moral leadership and independent political judgement in times of crisis. One inevitable result of choosing a head of state by inheritance rather than election is that in a crisis they may lack the confidence, popularity and independence needed to make any worthwhile contribution to the governance of Britain.

That is a pity, if only because the concept of an independent elected head of state is useful in a modern constitution, as one check on the power of a government which has no other checks and balances. It has no Upper House that it can't get round, no regional or state legislatures, not even a Greater London Council. It has no Supreme Court to pull it up short for violating the guarantees made to its citizens by a Bill of Rights.

The example of Mary Robinson in Ireland shows just how important it can be to have, even as a figurehead, an independent person above petty party politics. Someone who does at least embody the outlook that most people want to see projected onto the world stage as representative of their nation: a figure available to serve as leader in cases of government crisis or collapse. Good luck apart, the British monarchy will not provide – by sexist, racist, or religiously discriminatory descent – the calibre of leadership that can be provided by elections every seven years for a head of state.

I do, however, have a future in store for the monarchy. Let's keep it, in all its splendour and absurdity, as a living museum piece. Long may this royal soap opera run and run, long may New Zealand matrons scalp tickets to Buckingham Palace garden parties, long may *The Sun* compete with *The Mirror* to tell royal lies and half truths. Let's keep our kings and queens, our oaths of allegiance, and our whisky and jam and boot polish that comes 'by royal appointment'. Let's even keep our Queen's Counsel. But let us at long last write a constitution, and give the monarchy only a very small part in it. The Queen should be replaced as head of state for every practical purpose by a president, elected every five or seven years, who will make all the overseas state visits, advise the Government, inspire the people and open (and if necessary close) the Parliament.

There would be nothing to stop the monarch running for the presidency. In my own view, Prince Charles would make an excellent president. His chances of election would doubtless depend upon whether his ex-wife and his sister stood against him, as they would probably split the royal vote. We would then, perhaps end up with Kate Adie as president. And why not?

The answer, I suspect, lies in the forest of flowers sent to the Queen Mum whenever she is ill. It is an answer that suggests that the House of Windsor will provide our head of state for many years to come. This makes it all the more important that the ancient and rotting legal foundations of this state are rebuilt, and that the secular and minimal role of the monarch is clearly defined in a written constitution. At least that would give the monarchy a fighting chance of playing a useful part in the governance of twenty-first century Britain.

TOM PAULIN

MILTON – ONE OF US

IN A FAMOUS passage in his essay on *Coriolanus* William Hazlitt expresses this republican anxiety about the poetic imagination:

> The language of poetry naturally falls in with the language of power. The imagination is an exaggerating and exclusive faculty: it takes from one thing to add to another: it accumulates circumstances together to give the greatest possible effect to a favourite object. The understanding is a dividing and measuring faculty: it judges of things not according to their immediate impression on the mind, but according to their relations to one another. The one is a monopolising faculty, which seeks the greatest quantity of present excitement by inequality and disproportion; the other is a distributive faculty, which seeks the greatest quantity of ultimate good by justice and proportion. The one is an aristocratic, the other a republican faculty. The principle of poetry is a very anti-levelling principle. It aims at effect, it exists by contract. It admits of no medium. It is every thing by excess. It rises above the ordinary standard of sufferings and crimes. It presents a dazzling appearance. It shows its head turreted, crowned, and crested. Its front is gilt and blood-stained. Before it 'it carries noise, and behind it leaves tears'. It has its altars and its victims, sacrifices, human sacrifices. Kings, priests, nobles, are its train-bearers, tyrants and slaves its executioners – 'Carnage is its daughter' – Poetry is right-royal.

If the irrational theatre of monarchy has all the best images, how do those of us who believe and are empowered to say openly and without ridicule for the first time in many, many

178

generations – how do those of us who believe in a republic affirm the principle of the Republic of Great Britain? Perhaps first by saying that if the monarchy goes, so does the United Kingdom of Great Britain and Northern Ireland. England, Scotland and Northern Ireland will separate and set up republican forms of government.

England has a noble republican culture which was honoured and celebrated by French republicans during the French Revolution. Sadly, that culture is lost, buried, invisible. A figure like Algernon Sidney is scarcely remembered, while that fearless servant of English liberty, the first Earl of Shaftesbury, is subsumed by Dryden's savagely admiring caricature in *Absalom and Achitophel*.

But where and what are the images which express English republican culture? All that comes to mind is the statue of Cromwell outside the House of Commons, the great paintings of Burke's protégé, James Barr, in Burlington House, the mural showing the assassination of Julius Caesar in Chatsworth. Other than that there's nothing. Martin Amis, was surprised to learn that Milton, Wordsworth and James Joyce were republicans. This historical amnesia would appear to be representative of his generation – see also the long correspondence in the *London Review of Books* in 1985 when Milton's republicanism was explained to Craig Raine.

Our historical impoverishment became comically clear for me in 1988 when, in the historic heartland of the Glorious Revolution, the Chesterfield Constituency Labour Party issued an edict saying that the tercentenary of that revolution ought not to be celebrated. The daft left might have kept quiet because that anniversary passed with scarcely a whisper. The nation was not interested and the government did not want to draw attention to the Williamite Revolution. Would that the Chesterfield Constituency Labour Party had gone out and painted King William on the gable-ends of that town. The Orange habit might have spread throughout the land. Images of peaceful constitutional revolution could have proliferated and the old order might have started to break up – as it now is doing and will continue to do. Here, we must recognise that constitutional reform has to involve members of all the political parties. It is the Murdoch press which is giving the lead here and swinging a republican hammer against the walls of the House of Windsor.

If we in Charter 88 necessarily point to the now-perceived limitations and constitutional flaws which resulted from the ousting of the wretched Stuart dynasty, this does not preclude us from also celebrating the magnificent achievement of those courageous Whigs who gathered in Revolution House in Chesterfield to frame an invitation to King William. The lack of any national commemoration of that victory underlines the problems which an idealistic reform movement faces in finding ways of breaking open English history and culture in order to release those *imaginative* political energies which were last active in this country in the 1790s and for a period during the reign of Queen Victoria.

It is possible that if Australia becomes a republic in the near future then the different constituent parts of the United Kingdom will seek to throw off the degradation of those kitsch royalist images which have burdened the culture since the Restoration. If this happens, then the magic, the secrecy, the tight ethnic Anglican core of the state will be broken apart.

The Thatcher experiment promised to break the mould of British politics, but it burdened us instead with the archaic squalor of National Heritage – Sir John Gielgud and Prince Charles reciting the Lord's Prayer as they shunt a tank past Adlestrop. There is an alternative, a developing and modern heritage which is represented by this country's greatest non-dramatic poet, John Milton. These lines from the last book of that supreme republican epic, *Paradise Lost*, describe defeat at the hands of mystifying monarchists:

> Wolves shall succeed for teachers, grievous wolves,
> Who all the sacred mysteries of heaven
> To their own vile advantages shall turn
> Of lucre and ambition, and the truth
> With superstitions and traditions taint,
> Left only in those written records pure,
> Though not but by the Spirit understood.

Then shall they seek to avail themselves of names,
Places and titles, and with these to join
Secular powers, though feigning still to act
By spiritual, to themselves appropriating
The Spirit of God, promised alike and given
To all believers; and from that pretence,
Spiritual laws by carnal power shall force
On every conscience; laws which none shall find
Left them enrolled, or what the Spirit within
Shall on the heart engrave. What will they then
But force the spirit of grace itself, and bind
His consort liberty; what, but unbuild
His living temples, built by faith to stand,
Their own faith and conscience can be heard
Infallible? Yet many will presume:
Whence heavy persecution shall arise
On all who in the worship persevere
Of spirit and truth; the rest, far greater part,
Well deem in outward rites and specious forms
Religion satisfied; truth shall retire
Bestuck with slanderous darts, and works of faith
Rarely be found: so shall the world go on,
To good malignant, to bad men benign. . .

It is time to build the English Republic.

NEIL BELTON

A REPUBLIC OF THE IMAGINATION

IN HIS CONTRIBUTION to the monarchy debate, Tom Paulin quotes a very interesting passage from Hazlitt's essay on *Coriolanus*:

> The imagination is an exaggerating and exclusive faculty: it takes from one thing to add to another: it accumulates circumstances together to give the greatest possible effect to a favourite object. The understanding is a measuring and dividing faculty; it judges of things not according to their immediate impression on the mind, but according to their relations to one another. . . .The one is an aristocratical, the other a republican faculty.

Paulin rightly stresses that this is an expression of Hazlitt's 'republican anxiety' about the poetic imagination. Paulin urges us to rediscover what he believes to be a lost tradition of republican culture crowned by Milton, but what is really striking is how deeply we've inherited the assumption that imagination can't be republican, that understanding and science can't be imaginative. 'Poetry is right-royal', says Hazlitt: an apprehension of the emerging split between literature and the natural sciences, and a rueful sense that the highest culture mirrors in its concentration of linguistic force the untrammelled state power of absolutism. Later in the same essay Hazlitt uncharacteristically concludes: 'This is the logic of the imagination and the passions; which seek to aggrandize what excites admiration and to heap contempt on misery, to raise power into tyranny, and to make tyranny absolute. . .We

182

may depend upon it that what men delight to read in books, they will put in practice in reality.'

But there were and are ways of linking language and power (as Hazlitt's own wider doctrine of the sympathetic imagination showed) that don't turn poetry into the Genghis Khan of the arts, and which are untroubled by the pessimistic assumption that the imagination is inherently anti-democratic; nor has our culture been without alternative resources more recent than the seventeenth century. Leaving aside the traditions of Celtic republicanism, whose marginality is assumed in the deathless London trope of 'regional literature', North American writers' commitment to democracy and obsession with 'understanding' have not been kept completely offshore. Images of ambition and creativity in Melville and Whitman, for example, don't need the nimbus of kingship. Melville's rhapsodically democratic art found its highest expression in a book that fuses writing about nature, biology, language, sailing, desire and zoology; and it was English radical liberals and reformers in the 1860s and 70s who kept *Moby-Dick*'s reputation alive. James Thomson, William Morris, D.G. Rossetti, Charles Bradlaugh and Henry Salt (Thomson's first biographer) were among the dissidents who cultivated Whitman and Melville in the heyday of the Queen-Empress and ever-grander ceremonies of popular monarchism.

Yet Hazlitt's ironic contrast has become an actual cultural gulf in postwar Britain. It's there in the dead formula of 'the two cultures', in the well-bred refusal to be interested in 'stinks'; in the state withdrawing from research, in good physics professors earning less than apprentice lawyers, with emigration to California for the lucky and mobile ones. The 'republican faculty' is a shabby laboratory at the back of a national museum.

For the whole solemn crew of English literary ideologists who have set the tone of the national culture, from reactionary modernists like Eliot and Leavis to socialists like the early Raymond Williams and Richard Hoggart, it was evident that 'culture' is set against the mechanism, the determinism, the soul-death of scientific rationality. Arnold's essays are

Literature; Huxley's are unread. There is a pessimistic assumption that science is impenetrable, that it must be manipulative and frightening, that it is an uncontrollable Promethean force. Science since 1945 has been the perfect analogue of secret power – in Brecht's vision of an amoral research community, Pynchon's Rocket State, the infogothic jokes of Dr Strangelove and *Jurassic Park* (with Hawking as the Mekon's benign younger brother). As for the real stuff – pesticides, defoliants, cultured anthrax, toxic dumps, radiated steppes and map-reading bombs – it doesn't bear thinking about: all those bad risks built into the equations.

Like most dreams these nightmares have more than a passing connection with real threats, but to accept all of this as unchangeable is an abandonment of the democratic intelligence. For different things can be done with science, depending on what kind of markets and institutions set goals for it, and on how critically aware we, the nonspecialist people, choose to be about it. The heart-valve, the plastic hip, the fax machine and the existence of a cornucopia – by historical standards – in every Western vegetable shop are also consequences of scientific research. It is much easier for the military establishment to monopolize the greater part of a country's scientific effort if the electors are becalmed, when they contemplate technology, between wonder and fear. In short, we need a culture that values science, and a politics that allows democratic control over its capabilities. We have neither in Britain at the moment.

Indeed, the strangeness of Britain is highlighted by our almost literally constitutional inability to get excited about science. The time when people could invoke the names of Faraday, Darwin, Kelvin and Maxwell as symbols of great human achievements is already a hundred years old, the dream of progress they represented as archaic to us as the statues that exalt some of them as Great Men in a few public parks. There is no willed public memory of thinkers like Bragg, Rutherford or Dirac from early in our own century; no older archival piety either: Newton's *Principia* – the foundation of modern mechanics – is totally out of print in the UK. It's an odd country in which the word 'scientist' doesn't carry some connotation of respect for a person's dedication to hard learning and submission to a difficult standard of truth. Our only modern scientific icon is a gifted cosmologist whose work very few outside physics can appreciate, an image of suffering genius that stands in for science in the most mystifying way.

There are those who argue that talk about science is never going to be much more than that, in the late twentieth century: a mythology justifying power, science as the new religion of the world market. Science is so in thrall to technology, which is steeped in oppressive power relationships and is driven to repress human agency at every level from the workplace to the home, that it must be resisted – never celebrated. This is an apparently radical argument, breaking completely from the older facile socialist belief in science-as-progress and repelled by the drunken engineering of Stalinism. While it raises issues of huge importance about the social purpose and responsibility of both the market and of scientists researching for it, it also has its peculiarly British inflection in a tendency to repress all but the most critical lay reflection on science, to ban curiosity, excitement and exposition as mere 'gee-whizzery'. To be, in other words, profoundly hostile to science from the margins of science, often in terms indistinguishable from the heirs of Coleridge and Leavis. A more fruitful position is surely to insist that science offers compelling evidence of processes in a real, objective world - versions of 'the torn body of truth', in Milton's beautiful phrase from the *Areopagitica* – and that there is a necessary place for popular discussion of its theories precisely so that their effects can be better understood, and the more obvious it becomes that some global problems can only be solved by a combination of political action and scientific ingenuity, the more essential is a democratic culture of science. Colin Tudge argues in *The Engineer in the Garden* that 'the problems of Third World communities often demand much higher technologies than those of the affluent West.' The near future promises seeds resistant to specific pests, self-fertilising and high-yielding, but as Tudge points out, these technological riches are too expensive for poor farmers in Africa: enabling them to plant genetically-engineered sorghum becomes a vitally important question of politics and morality. Our need to know about the world has never been greater.

English culture's vision of itself is instead dangerously literary, romantic, nostalgic, deludedly 'poetic'; and its popular and political imagination has, over the past 40 years especially, collapsed into a literally 'royal' form of kitsch – a ghastly parody of Hazlitt's vision of poetry as aristocratic and steeped in the language of power. Indeed when our ancient form of state is defended it's often explicitly in terms of enchanting a heartless modern world: the monarchy as a bit of poetry in our dull lives. Charles Moore shows no trace of Hazlitt's unease about the state-forms of the mind: 'The realm of poetry and fancy is an important part of the life of any nation, and it is no accident that one calls it a realm, rather than a republic.' But it *is* an accident, sustained by three centuries of energetic compromise, a contingency of history that invocations of Georgian poetic phraseology can't protect from change. 'One' can also call the territory of the imagination a land, a country – even a republic of letters.

In these twilight years of the Glorious Revolution, the public temper and dignity of other kinds of imagination has been weakened; but not terminally. Most creative writers are too intelligent to buy into the semi-official contempt for mere science. More, clearly, is involved here than whether art and science have anything to say to or about each other (orthodox guardians of the crossroads like Professor Lewis Wolpert flatly deny that they do) or whether science can be the subject matter or inspiration of art (as it is so brilliantly in the work of writers as diverse as DeLillo, Banville, Hamilton-Paterson, Winterson and McEwan – to name only a few novelists). Thankfully, the very cast of mind that insists on the absolute separation of art and literature and science is under attack. As the disabling terms of the current orthodoxy become increasingly apparent, few would insist that the way to a non-monarchist culture lies in a revision of the literary canon.

Scientist-writers are, after all, staking a place in the wider culture: Steve Jones's Reith Lectures brought together human history and genetics in ways that illuminated both; the

American biologist Stephen Jay Gould has revived the scientific essay as a populist art-form that defends both the heritage of scientific rationality and illegitimate metaphorical extensions of it into human culture (the selfishness of the gene excusing the short-term greed of the City, as it were); Richard Dawkins is Britain's great militant atheist polemicist. These are not simply popularizers of science, they are putting central arguments into our culture and are read in this way by a public unimpressed by the narrow inherited categories.

Science has a realism which it's difficult to avoid, a feeling of knowledge becoming inescapable, sobering and exalting. Let me give on example. Reading *The Origin of the Species* for the first time remains an experience as worth recommending as a reading of *Paradise Lost*. The relentless courteous prose transforms our human sense of historical scale and our most comforting beliefs in the immutability of nature. Three thousand years of philosophical obsession with ideal essences is burned slowly away by the cautious unfolding of a simple argument. Even Darwin's burial in Westminster Abbey, which his most recent biographers see as his induction by the English establishment into a safe conservative pantheon, can't cancel the positive charge of this extraordinary book.

To deny that there is imagination - creativity, beauty of insight and synthesis – in evolutionary theory (or quantum theory, to take a harder case) is an exercise in willed cultural self-mutilation. These are among the most highly-elaborated forms of modern thought, with the capacity to unchain immensely powerful technologies. They are also intrinsically compelling and communicable, even if only for most of us in translations of mathematics into verbal language.

It is, I'd suggest, a shared realism and capacity to change the world through the open discussion of problems that makes a connection between science and democracy more than a woeful echo of Whig or Fabian dreams. Both science and democracy at their best share a willingness to be found wrong, to share information, to test themselves against reality. Of course there's no easy analogy between the consensual research programmes of genetics or particle physics and the fiercely contested priorities of politics in a divided society; and the violence, instability and irrationalism of the US are proof enough that democracy and enthusiasm for science do not in themselves guarantee a society that is sustainable or desirable. Science without a critical culture around it, and democracy without a social or moral consensus, are incomplete.

Yet the quite specific absence of open, rational, intelligible democratic standards in the UK is part of a culture that puts magic a long way before science and is therefore, paradoxically, very vulnerable to the unquestioned imperatives of technology.

There can be an imagination that isn't embarrassed by the ornate, antiquated barricades our culture has thrown up at every crossroads in the country, including some of the intellectual meeting points that should be most friendly and accessible. It will have many sources, not all of them lost or buried. We may find that the republican imagination has been at work for years in England, just that it's been invisible from the royal enclosure.

CAROLE TONGUE MEP

MAASTRICHT BLUES

A COLLEAGUE OF mine in the European Parliament said, when I asked about his view of our monarchy, 'There are monarchs and monarchs, some we can live with, but the British Royal Family and all the hangers-on are perhaps the worst example in Europe, and entrench so much that conflicts with a modern fair and just society.'

But will the British monarchy conflict *de jure* with the new Treaty or European Union? The concept of EC citizenship as set out in the Maastricht Treaty is limited and won't conflict with the monarchy to any great degree. For the EC institutions to become more democratic, the power of individual nation states and their governments should be exercised in partnership and equality with the European Parliament; there the monarch's role is of little or no significance. So the question really is, 'Does the British monarchy, as opposed to other monarchies in Europe, conflict with the development of a modern democracy based on equal citizenship and a more balanced distribution of wealth and power as enshrined as an aim in the EC treaties and in the Maastricht treaty?'

First, if one looks at the principle of equal opportunities and equal citizenship, the old inegalitarian features of the monarchy and the aristocracy should have no place in Britain today, which is still a viciously class-divided society. Fortunately or unfortunately, our monarchy is hopelessly ensnared in this, a symbol of inequality and inherited opulence.

Does our monarchy sit well with a modern multicultural society? I believe it is inappropriate in our multicultural society, and indeed the rest of the Community, that a monarch should be head of the Church of England. Indeed, a state church and a state religion should be abolished.

As regards democracy, the monarch still retains a number of powers known as the Royal Prerogative, which taken together amount to a potentially dangerous intrusion on the powers of the democratically-elected parliament and government. I don't believe the Royal Prerogative has any place in contemporary Britain. It should be eliminated as part of the overall move to a written constitution which defines not only the conditions under which a government holds office but also the fundamental rights of the British people. We are already living within a European written constitution which by 1996 will probably contain a section on human rights in any case.

As regards the correct and transparent use of public money, another feature of a modern democracy, the issue of the number of family members supported by the public purse is now one that has to be faced. This is a consequence of the personal scandals surrounding the Royal Family. In a reformed monarchy the number of those supported by public funds must be strictly limited. The vast wealth which makes the monarch one of the most powerful property-owners in Britain should be claimed by the state in the name of the British people. There is no reason at all why the head of the state should preside over such a huge private fortune whose existence has virtually nothing to do with the efforts or sagacity of the Royal Family, but rather has to do with the creation of wealth by the British people as a whole.

If we look at hereditary privilege, we have to look at the House of Lords. At the same time as the monarchy is being reformed it is quite clear to me that the House of Lords, the most absurd symbol of rule by the privileged in the whole of the democratic world, should be abolished and replaced by a democratic second chamber. It's the one thing that colleagues in other European countries completely fail to understand.

In a new constitution, a bill of individual and social rights should be enshrined, a bill that would encourage active citizenry and would abolish the arbitrary limits we have on free speech, freedom to publish, freedom of information. These limits have all too often marred and continue to mar Britain's democracy and make it look shabby alongside other democracies within the European Community, all of which have a written constitution. None of them, for example, would have allowed abolition of the GLC – 'an unbelievable attack on democracy', declared Michel Rocard at a recent London conference.

In such a new constitutional arrangement, where the people not the Crown are sovereign, there can be a place for a monarchy, if it can symbolise the equality of the British people. I don't believe there is any better model for such a monarchy than the so-called bicycle-riding monarchs of Scandinavia with their purely ceremonial roles. Such an apolitical monarch with no vested wealth or privilege could play a positive role as head of state acting as a unifying symbol for the British people. The question we have to leave open is, 'Can our monarchy be reformed and come to look like that?' But if the British people, and I emphasise it is they who need to decide, do so decide to keep a monarchy subject to democratic norms, then there is no reason for this to be incompatible with the European Union.

VERNON BOGDANOR

THE QUEEN AND EUROPE

MONARCHY AND EUROPE, comprises two aspects. The first is the relationship between the monarchy and the European Union: the second is the working of the Continental monarchies.

In the House of Lords, in February 1993, Lord Tebbit asked whether the Maastricht Treaty imposed new duties or obligations upon the Queen or affected the constitutional position of the monarchy. The reply, quite rightly, was that it neither imposed new duties, nor did it affect the constitutional position of the monarchy.

The Queen has the same rights as any other European citizen under Articles 8 to 8e of the Maastricht Treaty, but she is not compelled to exercise them. If one looks at Articles 8 to 8e of the Maastricht Treaty – the so-called Citizenship Chapter – this gives various rights to citizens, additional to but not a substitute for, those one already has as citizens of Britain, France or Germany.

The only duty it imposes is the general obligation to obey Community law but that is not a problem for most people because Community law in general imposes obligations upon governments, public bodies and companies rather than upon individuals. It affects individuals mainly through trading relationships. The Queen is hardly involved in these.

The only new rights that the Citizenship Chapter provides are new voting rights to residents of member states of which they are not nationals. Thus, French or German citizens now have rights to vote in British local elections and British elections to the European Parliament. Similarly, if any British citizen goes to live in France, or any other Community member state, he or she can then vote in their local elections or elections to the European Parliament and also become a candidate.

These new rights are hardly relevant to the Queen who resides in Britain. Moreover, even if the European Union were to give the Queen further rights, any rights she exercised would be at her discretion, and that discretion presumably would be exercised upon the advice of her ministers. So Maastricht in no way alters the role of the Queen nor of our constitutional monarchy, nor does it alter the role of the Sovereign of any other of the countries of the Community which are monarchies. It is worth remembering that six of the twelve member states are monarchies. Apart from Britain, they are Belgium, Denmark, Luxembourg, the Netherlands and Spain.

But the real question of interest is a much wider one than this very limited constitutional aspect – it is, what happens to the Queen if the Community becomes a federal state? Before answering this question, however, there is a preliminary question that needs to be answered. It is – what do we mean by federal?

One answer might be – a country like the United States. Were Europe to become federal in this sense, then Britain would become like Texas or Alabama, New York or Connecticut, and the Queen would be roughly in the position of the Governor of one of these states. She would enjoy merely local powers like the legislature of Texas or Alabama or New York.

It is true that the word federal is frequently used about the European Union, but nobody really believes that Europe in the near future will become like the United States of America. The term 'federal' when applied to the European Union is used in a different sense.

So far, the Union comprises mainly commercial and economic powers. Maastricht transfers more powers to the Union. But it does not really have a common defence or foreign policy – Bosnia has shown that – and so it is far from being a state in any traditional sense. A federal Europe in the sense in which we talk about a federal United States is unlikely to come about for hundreds of years, if ever. And even if it did, people would probably still need symbols of national identity, and so the monarchy would remain an important institution.

What has happened is that, as powers have been transferred from Westminster to Brussels, Britain has lost some of her sovereignty. There are certain things that Parliament can no longer do in the economic and commercial field. For example, Parliament could no longer, if it wished, impose a tariff on goods from France, Germany or other member states of the Union.

Therefore, the Queen, as head of state, presides over a country which has less sovereignty over its own affairs. Thus, while her formal powers and influence remain the same, they are exercised over a smaller area. One might argue that the prerogative covers less, but of course ninety five percent of the prerogative powers are in fact exercised by ministers, so this is really a problem for ministers much more than a problem for the Queen. The question that ministers have to answer is – are they happy to have powers transferred from Parliament to Brussels. That of course is a political question and different people have different views on it. But the question is not really relevant to the debate on the monarchy. In fact, whether one is in favour of European integration or not, the monarchy ought to be kept out of the issue, just as it should be kept out of other policy issues.

But there is a final issue related to Europe, a matter of style. In the past, the British monarchy has been focused not only on Britain but also upon another forty nine countries of the Commonwealth. The Queen is, of course, Head of the Commonwealth, and also Queen of sixteen other countries within the Commonwealth. It may be that if British policy comes to focus more on Europe than on the Commonwealth, then also the focus of the monarchy will change so that it becomes more of a European monarchy and perhaps less of a Commonwealth monarchy. It may mean that new forms of symbolism need to be developed with regard to the monarchy. That may not be as difficult as it seems because the identification of the Queen with the Commonwealth is comparatively recent. The present Queen is the first Head of the Commonwealth, a new title invented in the late 1940's, and the association of the Queen with the Empire, which preceded the Commonwealth is also comparatively recent. It is less than 120 years since Queen Victoria became Empress of India in 1876. That was a consequence of Disraeli's imperialist policy, identifying the monarchy with Empire, something much resented by the Liberal opposition.

Obviously, the Queen cannot become Empress of Europe. But perhaps there might be some alternative symbolism if we move closer toward European integration. Monarchy is essentially an institution of the imagination. It is difficult to analyse because it appeals not so much to the intellect as to the imagination. We all need symbols in our lives, we need to use our imaginations. Disraeli understood that in the nineteenth century, and he strengthened the monarchy by identifying it with the developing Empire. It was a brilliant act of imaginative politics.

Can we find a modern Disraeli who can identify the monarchy with more modern concerns and perhaps in particular with the European Community? That is the problem. Is there a Disraeli who can revivify the monarchy, and, if so, where is he or she to be found?

Finally, it is of some interest to look at the working of monarchy in other European countries. The monarchies of the Continent are Belgium, Denmark, Luxembourg, Netherlands and Spain, and also Norway and Sweden currently outside the Community. These countries are amongst the most stable and prosperous countries of Europe and a number of them are identified with policies of radical egalitarianism. If one looks for democratic socialism in action, one looks to Sweden, Norway and Denmark. This refutes the superficial view that the monarchy prevents radical change by encouraging deference. Indeed one can argue that the monarchy in countries such as Denmark, Norway and Sweden has performed an important function of accommodating people to change because, in an era of radical change people need existing landmarks.

All these countries, except for Britain, have codified constitutions, and they also all have proportional representation. Contrary to what many constitutional reformers believe, the existence of a constitution does not actually make much difference to the role of the monarchy because it defines the working of the monarchy in purely formal terms. For example, if one looks at the Dutch constitution, it says 'the King appoints and dismisses ministers'. That is purely formal. It does not say anything about the process by which ministers happen to be appointed. In any country, with a constitution or without, one has to rely upon conventions.

The nature of monarchy differs very subtly in every country. It is an inherently national institution, very difficult to generalise about. There is a different style in every country. The first thing most people notice about the Scandinavian monarchies is that they are bicycling monarchies. Some believe that Britain too should have a bicycling monarchy. But people also say that the Scandinavian countries are dull. We like the element of colour in government. It is a mistake to make government too dull. It is not easy, therefore, even within Europe to generalise about something inherently national and relating so deeply to national feelings and emotions as the monarchy.

WILL HUTTON

A Monarchy Economy

BRITAIN IS DIFFERENT. The configuration of our political, economic and social institutions marks them out as apart from those in the rest of Europe. If they worked well, if the country was prospering then there would be no cause for concern. But they do not.

More than that, there are powerful and compelling forces leading to European integration. Whatever setbacks lie along the way, Europe is constructing a constitution that will both have a supra-national competence and require democratisation. Nor is this the result of a muddled enthusiasm for things European, but reflects real interests. Whether it is safeguarding the environment, improving the regulation of the financial markets or rationalising their defence industries, the peoples of Europe have to act in concert with each other. The European construction reflects real needs.

There is no choice for Britain other than to participate in the process but it will demand root and branch changes in the British system. Integration must go further because European states are increasingly compelled by the logic of geography and interests to govern in concert and surrender competence to European institutions. The question is not Europe right or wrong, as the Conservative Europhiles have it; but Europe right or left.

They are correct on a European scale, wrong on a British one. Integration, even around a right-of-centre policy programme, poses Britain uniquely with a crisis of adaptation. The configuration of our economic, political and social

197

institutions is so different from those in Europe that integration beyond today's level will demand little less than a transformation of the British system. The Eurosceptics in both main political parties are surely right to argue that this has never been made plain; nor has there ever been an invitation to vote on it.

For those who believe, as this writer does, that the movement towards a transparent political constitution, regulated capitalism and a strong system of solidarity between classes is the key to prosperity and the good life, the European project is full of promise and adventure. The reforms that Europe will demand of us are precisely those we need to make to prevent the fragmentation of our society, the locking of our economy into a low-wage, low-skills equilibrium and rule by an 'opted-out' elite. European integration and the modernisation of Britain are two sides of the same coin – and if put to the vote would surely win a solid majority.

This can hardly be the view of a British Conservative. All the biases in the British system, from its media through the funding of political parties to the power of the business lobby, favour Conservatism. Capture 40 per cent of the popular vote and there is complete control of the state doling out favours, patronage and running great departments of state as mini-fiefdoms. To limit this in any way, even at the margin, is hard indeed.

The Conservative party is a construct of the particular set of British political institutions. A singular notion of sovereignty informs its political philosophy. The state power it enjoys has formed its character. The British system does not require political parties to share power or seek consensus, giving them an experience of doing political business as it is done on the European mainland; instead it confers on the governing party the authority to do what it wills. For the Conservatives this is one of the essential components of their make-up.

Nor is it an accidental outgrowth of history. The sovereignty exercised by the governing party in the House of Commons is monarchical in its roots. It is unqualified precisely because of its regal character. Monarchs do not brook checks and balances, and once the governing party has a majority in the House of Commons neither does it. It governs quasi-regally, arrogating the prerogative powers once held by the Crown.

Yet the model of regulated capitalism around which Europe organises its integration has as its fountainhead a model of governance which is participative and decentralised. The state embodies the commonwealth. It is an instrument of the people. There are mediating public institutions between the state and the individual. The state regulates capitalism and sets boundaries in the people's name. Of course the dirty waters of politics demand compromises, fixes and deals which are no more noble than those arrived at in Britain or anywhere else; but the origin of political legitimacy is different and this intrudes into every nook and cranny of European life. In Britain sovereignty is unqualified because its origins are royal; in Europe sovereignty is qualified because its origins are democratic.

And that is where the differences begin. The British never set out to industrialise as the mainland Europeans have done, deliberately developing institutions to further economic modernisation; instead, industrialisation happened apparently spontaneously without state involvement. The European tradition of regulated capitalism has no counterpart in Britain.

Equally, there is only a weak British tradition for building institutions of social solidarity as an act of self-interest for the middle class. The British welfare state was created by the labour movement in the face of Conservative scepticism not as a country-wide expression of social solidarity. The middle class has never experienced strong totalitarian parties of right and left building a political base upon the discontents of the working class, as has happened in mainland Europe. It does not feel that it needs to protect its freedoms with a larger framework that encompasses the population as a whole. The middle class sees its privileges as natural rights – certainly not in need of defending and legitimising by loyalty to a wider social settlement.

Institutions of social solidarity and economic modernisation can take on a bewildering variety – just to mention some shows how deep the fissures run between Britain and its European partners. From the notion of the firm and its place in society to systems of child care, Britain stands apart.

Start with the labour market. The British now boast 10,000 points where wages are determined; 22 per cent of the labour force is in part-time jobs; trade unions have never been considered as 'social partners'. This increasingly casualised labour force is not deemed to be a potential stake-holder in the enterprises in which it works. The Germans and Swedes can co-ordinate wage bargains by striking deals between big unions and industry associations; worker participation in decision-making is taken as read. Britain does not possess that capacity, and never has.

Instead, stake-holding in enterprise is encouraged by the ownership of shares either directly, or indirectly via the savings institution. The financial system is not seen as a place where the nation's savings are channelled into its economic development via a complex of industrial investment banks and long-term shareholders; rather it is a market place where savers shop around for the highest return.

But this is only the tip of the iceberg. Take home ownership. Owner occupation in Britain is close to 70 per cent; in Germany 45 per cent. But more important, 90 per cent of Britain's nine million mortgage holders have floating-rate debt, compared with less than 10 per cent in Germany and France. Europe's politicians are unfamiliar with the agonies faced by their British counterparts over the political consequences of changes in short-term interest rates. Their fixed-rate mortgage holders are unaffected and in any case not so indebted; whether it is their own central bank or a possible European Central Bank raising interest rates, they do not understand the political fall-out accompanying such action in Britain.

And so it goes on. The British offer such a low state pension that private provision is a necessity; the Europeans are more generous. The British education system, with its emphasis on educating the elite through private schools and neglecting the education of the majority, is again by European standards a curiosity. Organising and funding a public system of vocational training on the scale of Germany is unthinkable.

Nor does the state organise a system of national child-care that underwrites the position of children while women work; Britain's child-care spending is the lowest in Europe. Again, while the middle class accepts that both nursery education and quality child-care are proper for its own children, there is no readiness to accept a solidarity of interest with the rest of society.

The tradition of a common or public interest is negligible but then Britain does not possess the constitution that expresses public purpose. As the Eurosceptics point out, the House of Commons is sovereign; it is the instrument of the majority party to further its will, not the place where a common interest is expressed and hammered out.

Thus, the Eurosceptics are right about the profundity of the changes required if Britain is to be 'at the heart of Europe' but surely wrong to insist that the changes should be resisted. Britain's antediluvian structures are a problem: whether or not it integrates with Europe.

The system must be seen in its totality. It hangs together as a whole. The lack of social citizenship which stands behind the inability to construct a durable social settlement; the lack of political citizenship which underpins the incapacity to express a common interest; and the lack of economic citizenship which makes it impossible to incorporate the firm as a web of rights and obligations, all have the same roots. They are all bound up one in another.

And for this Britain must look to its unwritten constitution and the nature of power that it permits. If the state incorporates no other conception of power but absolute executive discretion there should be no surprise that in the private domain the same notion is copied. The executive boss swaggering at his untrammelled power is literally copying what he sees in the political sphere; the legal structures are the same, so is the culture and so is the reality. The lack of common interest which implies an underfunded rail system has the same roots as the system of corporate governance which allows directors to walk away from ailing companies with millions in their pockets.

Thus no effective, lasting change is possible without addressing our political system; and no fundamental change to that is possible without changing its monarchical foundations and writing down the responsibilities and competence of the Crown. Until political power is checked and shared, Britain cannot legally begin renewal; there are simply not the constitutional and political building blocks.

This does not mean a republic, necessarily. But it does mean a republican attitude to the constitution. There are good reasons in a changing world to preserve a landmark that has survived a millennium; but there are no reasons to retain it as an obstacle to reforming our polity, society and economy to suit the life we live today. We must rethink what we want from the Crown. The objective is citizenship; without it there is no avenue to economic renewal, social cohesion or modernising our democracy.

ELIZABETH LONGFORD

Phoenix From The Windsor Ashes

WHEN I WAS researching the life of Queen Victoria, I was rather surprised to find that, after the death of Albert, whenever she got into a real row with her ministers, her immediate reaction was to say, 'I'll abdicate, I shall go to Australia'. I don't think today that's the country she would choose.

Now we are seeing the same kind of rumpuses and crises that have beset the British monarchy throughout its career. Just as it surmounted all the past ones, many of them a great deal more serious than anything that has happened today, which have been personal matters, I firmly believe that it will surmount this one.

When my recent book on the Royal Family was being prepared my publishers were kind enough to allow me to make suggestions for the jacket design. The book was published in April 1993. In the circumstances I wanted to have the flaming ruins of Windsor Castle in the background and in the foreground the very delightful portrait of the Queen smiling and the symbol I thought everybody would get would be that this was the phoenix, the royal phoenix rising from the ashes and flames of disaster.

Not everybody got that symbolism. My friend A N Wilson, who also brought out a book around the same time, looked at the jacket and said 'I know why the Queen is smiling. It was she who put the match to the wing of Windsor Castle, and she put it for the insurance money'. Well, let that pass.

My point is that the symbol of the phoenix still has its

relevancy but in fact it is Prince Charles above all who has got to be the phoenix of the future, and rise from the flames which have been licking him in different aspects of his career.

To me there is no question whatsoever that his is the future of the monarchy, if it has one. It simply cannot be Princess Diana's in any circumstances. The idea of two courts, two rival courts, is a sham. It cannot exist. It does not make sense. It will not exist.

Princess Diana can do her public work, which I am sure everyone admires tremendously. I certainly do. She has almost magical gifts. She says that she can smell suffering a mile off and in that sense she means she has a kind of intuition of the people who need help and sympathy. She can perfectly well go on doing that and I am quite sure she will. After all there are millions of people in this country with a sense of public service. You don't need to have a court in order to help people, and smell suffering and go into hospitals and stand up for people with Aids. You can be public spirited and an individual person and that is what I think will happen.

If Princess Diana remarries, as I am sure she will, her only connection will be as mother of a future king. If Prince William is made a back door for her re-entry to power that would be a fatal development. I feel pretty sure it won't happen.

On the most basic argument, why should anybody assume that because we had the tragedy and sorrow of Squidgygate and Camillagate there would not be other 'gates'? Why assume there would not be a Williamgate or even a Harrygate? We cannot look forward into the future and just because they are two innocent little school boys now, it does not mean that when we have upset the whole constitution, got rid of the proper heir, we are going to have somebody who has no faults at all and has a little angelic halo around his head for the rest of his life. It does not make sense. I am quite sure it will not happen.

Prince Charles himself could remarry – this is very much in the balance. Sometimes I think he will and sometimes I think he won't. We just don't know. But if he does there will certainly be a problem, but in my opinion it will be the problem of the Church of England. It won't be his problem. Perhaps the Church will borrow another leaf out of Henry VIII's book and try the solution of annulment. In the church that I belong to, the Roman Catholic Church, we do have annulment. To my amazement, I did not know that the Anglican Church does not have annulment even though its founder, Henry VIII, used it lavishly, just as lavishly as he used the chopping block on Tower Hill. So I just offer that quite freely as an idea that might be mulled over.

Prince Charles will have need of one thing very much indeed, but one thing only. And that is that when the time comes the people of this country should want him. I mean seriously that whatever the obstacles, whether you call them constitutional or whatever else they're called, if the people of this country say he is going to be our next monarch, they will have him. The monarch was made for the people and the people will have their choice and they will make it.

I will just mention three reasons why I think they will stand behind him.

First of all there is a natural loyalty in this country towards the heir. That loyalty can be strained and broken as it was towards Edward VIII. People would not believe it possible, but I was alive then and old enough to see the amazing way in which the loyalty of the country was simply, quietly and smoothly transferred from King Edward VIII to King George VI. But that was because they were not satisfied with the former. Prince Charles' good qualities are admirably suited, as I see it, to a democratic monarch. First of all his social work, which he is totally involved in, and sincerely minds about and works out and cares about; and he has the right attitude I think to social work. He doesn't go to either extreme. He is not a collectivist but he is a great believer in co-operative work. The motto of one of his projects is 'We will do it together' and that is the right attitude in this country. At the same time he gets very bored and fed up with red tape, which makes him see red as one might say, and therefore he is in between, he sees the values of collectivism and the values of individual enterprise.

Again, his mind is original. Some people could call it a bit freakish or eccentric. I don't look on it like that. But he is interested in forward looking ideas. Perhaps you could say carried away by them. It doesn't matter. He is not king yet. It's a good thing for him to try out a great number of things provided that they are things for his future citizens, whose king he is going to be; I will not use the word subjects because it's a word that republicans try and use against us quite wrongly. His interest in the environment, in ecology, in the greens, all that kind of thing, is simply amazing for a future king. And if we have a king who has that kind of attitude we will be extremely lucky.

Lastly, I think he will be chosen because there is an instinctive dislike of the idea of a president especially as every English person that I know, every British person I should say, automatically assumes that the president would be a retired out-of-date politician, and that is the last thing they want. They don't want any retired handbags, they don't want any retired old tobacco pipes; they want somebody who is out of politics, who has never been in politics, who is above politics, above social groups, above social classes, and therefore they are not in favour of a president. And the republicans themselves play into this hand by not being the least bit serious as they used to be in the old days. There is no serious republican movement here. They are all quite friendly and nice people.

DAVID HARE

GUTS OR GARTERS

NOW THAT THE dust is settling, historians have fallen to arguing about the most significant legacy of the Thatcher years. The barrage of trendy rhetoric which marked out her period of government no longer disguises the widening gap in this country between the rich and the poor, nor indeed the wave of crime and violence that gap has generated. The spiteful hostility towards those who give their lives to public services, and the attack on the idea of professionalism itself, are seen in our law courts, our schools and our hospitals to have taken a terrible toll. Yet nothing Mrs. Thatcher left behind her seems to me more lasting and more damaging than the widespread belief that we cannot alter the structure of institutions to serve people better.

Ironically, it is the British monarchy which now finds itself the most eminent victim of this fashionable neglect of structural change. Of all British institutions, it suddenly appears one of the sickliest. During the eighties, the Queen enjoyed a considerable popularity in the country at large by letting it be known how concerned she was at the wrenching effects of government policy on the social fabric of her kingdom. Like the Church, she assumed an oppositional role, tacitly making it clear that she disapproved of her own ministers' priorities. Just as monarchy traditionally finds a purpose during a war, so the House of Windsor prospered under Mrs. Thatcher's army of occupation. But now that times have changed and we need instead to be picking up the pieces, the Palace has woken into a nightmare. No-one can quite remember why it is there.

It is pointless to complain, as some have done, that the Palace has not thought enough about its so-called 'role'. Like many things in life, it exists in order to continue to exist. Most of the Palace's actions, which commentators affect to find incomprehensible, are in fact quite clearly tailored to ensure its own survival. Its doors, for instance, have not been opened so that it may share its wealth. It has a much simpler aim. It wants to be richer and better liked. But the Palace is not by any means just the blind organism of popular science. It also has a brain. And inside that brain it retains an ideology so palpably out of tune with the beliefs and ideas of its citizens that it chooses to keep silent rather than to open itself to public incredulity.

Would-be reformers of the Royal Family who think that it can be tinkered into the present day would do well to address the problem of the divine right of kings. Although it is not said in public, it is an inconvenient fact for all those who would like to see a 'modern monarchy' that the Queen, Prince Philip and Prince Charles are still devout believers in this ancient doctrine. They believe that they rule by right. Plainly they have made an accommodation with the elected representatives of the state. They know to bide their time and button their lips. But never have they publicly yielded an inch in their underlying claim that they are there because God wishes them to be.

It is this basic turn of mind – the country is theirs not in trust, but by right – which has lately given the monarchy its peculiarly sullen character. It is commonly complained that this royal house has lacked imagination. There are no great public projects. There are no new parks. There are no huge endowments for medicine or education. There are no commissions to first-rate sculptors, nor any signs of shame or responsibility that our best architects are all forced to work abroad. But these familiar accusations are not, as they are usually presented, charges against individuals who are by nature stupid or mean-spirited. They are reflections of an ideology which has had its day. The House of Windsor has not bothered to be generous because, literally, it does not see why it needs to be.

It is only by understanding how profound is their belief in

208

their own rights that we may make any sense of their attitudes, and realise how doomed, therefore, is any project of reform. Defenders of the Crown see its future in terms of some sort of balancing act between public access and private distance. But the fabled mystique, said to be essential to a monarchy's survival, is now little more than a technique for trying to hide from us what they truly believe. When the Palace's friends argue that it may improve its 'image' by recruiting its circle from society at large, they do not seem to understand that it is only the traditional aristocracy which lives at ease with the Queen's own most fundamental assumptions, and that same aristocracy is having troubles with its gene pool. When the Queen makes her touching complaint that 'nobody invites us for the weekend any more', it is not simply the cry of someone trapped in the odious rituals of deference. It is a recognition that water is lapping round the edges of the class which thinks as she does.

For myself I have no doubt that we need an early referendum, allowing a sane debate about the abolition of the monarchy. When it is said that our Royal Family is the envy of foreigners, I have always noticed that what foreigners particularly like is that it is ours and not theirs. It is not a pleasant prospect to have to wait for another war before the monarchy rediscovers a sense of purpose. When John Major calls for a classless society, then clearly it cannot be achieved without first removing this fountainhead of falsity and snobbery. But even to put John Major's name near the word 'abolition' is to realise how far down the path we have gone towards believing ourselves to be powerless to change anything.

This sense of public impotence is very dangerous. We know in our hearts that the monarchy is a historical absurdity. But because we lack the courage to abolish it (as indeed we lack the courage for any radical undertaking), instead we are taking out our anger at our own bad faith by torturing the individuals involved. Newspapers, led by the Murdoch group, have begun the project of putting the Royal Family in such a state of tension that their lives will become unliveable. The pleasure they are taking in this does nobody credit. Because we do not have the guts to sweep the monarchy away, instead, like the powerless critics we have become, we shall do the only thing we dare. We shall mock them till they wish they had never been born.

MARINA WARNER

THE SLIPPED RETINA

WHEN JOHN MAJOR told the House of Commons on 9 December 1993 that the separation of Charles from his wife would have no constitutional repercussions, there was an audible silence in the chamber. Charles's future as head of the Church of England would not be affected, the Prime Minister went on, his children's ranking in the succession to the throne would be unaltered, and – this was the statement that then caused a sharp, collective intake of breath – 'there was no reason why the Princess of Wales should not be crowned Queen.'

The country has experienced to its cost the Prime Minister's uninquiring turn of mind. This declaration ran true to character; it presented wishes as facts, like a hopeful conjuror at a six year old's birthday party. In this case, there was probably no one who believed him. The body politic's afflictions were made plain by his assertions, not by the personal unhappiness of Diana or Charles or the children, or the opportunistic bargaining of both parties with their syco-phants among the press, not even by the prospect of parallel, His'n'Hers coronations, royal households, staffs etc, or the howling of the quasi-republicans among the papers, or the blow to popular adulation of the Royals.

All these factors opened up cracks in the building, and have a part to play in the crisis. But above all, by closing the question before it had even been put, let alone discussed, the Prime Minister revealed how little we know and are allowed to know about the monarchy today, about its influence, its relation to the organs of government, its powers, its responsibilities. As the obedient mouthpiece of the royal proclamation, Major allowed the public a glimpse of the non-collaborative character of the monarchy: the Queen's loyal subjects are not expected to have a say. The Prime Minister read the Palace statement, and Parliament was supposed to accept it.

The Queen, responding to the crisis, soon decided to pay taxes and removed some of the members of her family from the Civil List. However, welcome as the decision was, it is interesting that it was not aired in Parliament before the fact, but was announced by the Palace and received with gratitude as if it were a spontaneous and generous gift.

When the demands of Charter 88 were drawn up five years ago, the question of the monarchy was avoided. The founder members wanted to campaign for the reform of British democracy, they were acting on the urgent need to rebuild institutions, but the taboo surrounding the royal head of state was keenly felt. It was important to wait for the right moment, when people – from loyal subjects to aspiring citizens – could not refrain any longer from taking part in imagining what kind of a society we want. Bagehot considered that Great Britain had been, since 1832, a republic – a 'disguised' one. He argued that the monarchy was a necessary fiction, which offered 'a visible symbol of unity'. The moment has now come to examine what this arrangement implies and whether, as fiction, as disguise, as symbol, it meets the nation's needs.

Many people feel deep anxiety about 'attacking' the monarchy – and holding it up for scrutiny is feared to be an 'attack' – because it appears to embody the country itself as a spiritual entity, to personify the imaginary homeland of being British.

The Royals still possess mythic personae, however much we have now eavesdropped on their bedroom talk, learned of their personal eating habits and witnessed their fights; they are still hedged in divinity, their bodies sacralised by etiquette, their lives secrets to be stolen or vouchsafed. Republicanism in Australia was radically strengthened, not by the abandonment of Commonwealth interests in favour of the EC, but by

212

indignation at the wild anti-Australian uproar in the UK tabloids when Keating presumed to touch the Queen.

The word myth in common usage means a lie, as well as a higher truth. Myths tell stories and these stories are variously received, as blatant deceptions, as consoling fabrications, as inspiring higher truths. At the end of the *Republic*, Plato, who on the whole opposed all fictions, ends by declaring that maybe, somewhere, there is a saving myth. If the right myth can be woven, the right story told, the body politic will flourish. The British monarchy meets the conditions of myth, as romance and ideal, as symbol of unity and embodiment of nation, and its hold on the imagination, not just in this country, but all over the world, reveals the power of that myth.

Myths present themselves as eternal truths, but they are born in certain historical circumstances and grow, flourish or wither in relation to social change: this is probably one of the lessons of the past that offers the most hope, since it implies that we are not forever stuck in an endless narrative loop, like characters in an arcade video game which has run out of money. Some of the most exciting new work by historians like David Cannadine and Linda Colley has unfolded how many of the rituals surrounding kingship and affirming its relation to the national psyche have been recent innovations: the sons and daughters of Queen Victoria were married privately, in the family chapel with a few close relatives and friends in attendance. Only during this recent phase of the house of Windsor have the weddings been huge public ceremonies, claiming to erase differences and malaise in the joyous communal sharing of a fairy tale. Similarly, Edward VII was the first monarch to lie in state, in 1910, while the public filed past his bier in St Stephen's Hall, Westminster: what seemed a medieval custom, fitting for a sacred king in the necropolis of his forebears, was in fact a brand new notion.

Royal show biz has increased not only in the liturgy but also of course in the mass media, and in spite of the simulation of ordinariness and access (the 'walkabout' and the TV films about life at Balmoral), the public show disguises an increase in secrecy; the display of royal symbols, material and personal, masks a reluctance to unhedge the divinity. It is for instance difficult even to obtain verification from the Palace about pictures in the Royal Collection (which in fact do not all form part of the Queen's personal estate but belong to the nation) as well as to assess the amount of her wealth. By contrast, when George IV died, and his successor was to be crowned, it was discovered that the coronation robes were missing. They had been bought by Madame Tussaud's, at the sale of his personal effects at Phillips, in Bond Street in 1831. This story may be apocryphal, but pre-Victorian attitudes to royal pomp certainly differed from today's: after two hours of his brother's funeral, the new king, William IV, felt enough was enough and left before the close.

This does not of course represent a better state of royal affairs, but it does serve to show that far from being an unchanging and traditional fixture, the repository of ancient ideas of nation and identity, the monarchy is always being reshaped, the myth of royalty recast. The kings of France could be watched at meals: after mass on Sunday at Versailles the Royal Family ate in public. Later, Louis XVIII revived the rite, in an effort to restore the ways of the *ancien régime*. James Fenimore Cooper joined the crowd one day, paid his few francs to look at 'le grand couvert' of the king, and was shocked at the abject gazing of the people, their heads turning like sun-flowers, he noted. The Queen could propose that she and her family assemble at table for the visitors to Buckingham Palace and charge the public to see them in person, and it would certainly help towards the cost of the Windsor fire. But would it be desirable, acceptable, appropriate? Ideas about decorum change, as can ideas about the duties of heads of state in a democracy.

When Charles's separation was announced, many news-papers carried headlines about the end of the fairy tale. One of the functions of the Royal Family was to hold up to the public 'a presentation of ourselves behaving well', as Rebecca West once put it. Part of the consecration of modern monarchy derives from Queen Victoria's personal spectacle of domestic virtue. From the Jubilee of 1887 onwards, Britain's international prestige appeared refracted in her edifying widowhood and her prolific dynasty: benevolent and civilised authority personified by a single family. The introduction of personal ethics created complications for all her successors, notably Edward VIII, but never more so than today. The monarchy that is deemed to have no political power falls back on moral authority. The display of royal waxworks at Madame Tussaud's illustrate this very well: in the earlier part of the century, tableaux illustrated Great Moments and Great Deeds in the history of the nation, including King John signing the Magna Carta and the acceptance of sovereignty by the young Princess Victoria ('I will be good'). But today, the Royals must not be seen to be doing anything the least bit political, so their waxworks just stand in a family group, in evening dress and full decorations and face out, beaming. They are among the very few figures in the Museum who are cordoned off and therefore can't be included in a family snapshot. They are also suffering the consequences of mythological breakdown, and have had to be rearranged in the light of recent events. So the Duchess of York, still beaming, now stands perilously near the brink of the dais, and Charles and Diana have been parted and posed in different spaces, also still smiling.

The British monarchy weathered the revolutions of the continent in the eighteenth and nineteenth centuries, and, welcoming fugitive kings and queens in fear for their lives ever since, offered a dream of stability unknown elsewhere in Europe. This exemplariness was underpinned by belief in British constitutionalism and democracy and guaranteed by the perceived unimpeachability of the Royals themselves; the two disparate themes were tangled together in the mythic presence of the monarch, and demanded obeisance. The culture of deference, vigorously analyzed by social commentators like Piers Brendon (*Our Own Dear Queen*) and Tom Nairn (*The Enchanted Glass*), flourished on these twin myths of royal rectitude at the apex of an unassailable political structure. Such acquiescence is always offering complacency the other cheek: subjects and rulers in a mute and inert tableau.

'One's betters know best' isn't necessarily a British habit of mind, a kind of London fog affecting the nation's brain. It is, however, interwoven with institutional structures, with the lack of a participatory, vocal culture of citizenship. The problem has been aggravated by political stagnation of the last decade. We the public have become a kind of pea under a huge pile of mattresses. We can feel its dead weight, as well as the weight of the sleeper at the top, whose presence doesn't perhaps add greatly to the burden, but counts for something.

Myths are a lens with which to look at afflictions: they can act like burning glass, concentrating passions and morals as in a Greek tragedy, like a magnifier, exaggerating hopes and desires, as some pop idols do. They can also suffer, like the eye, from a detached retina, and then, little to nothing can be seen through the lens any more. The present monarchy has become detached from the present needs of the country over which it rules; but the disappointment, even dismay its members inspire as individuals should not obscure the problem with the structure of the institution itself. The idea that it offers a symbol of national unity itself depends on historical circumstances, and these have been changing rapidly and profoundly.

The sacred myth of timeless and undifferentiated national unity once conveyed by the monarchy can no longer be made to work for the British citizen, nor is it certain that it would be desirable even if it were feasible, since it was forged from historical oppositions (to enemies overseas, to the Popish church) that can only contribute to a dangerous insularity. The modern monarchy rose to its apogee of popular strength with the rise of nation-states from the eighteenth century onwards, and this too has been changing fast in the new Europe, tossed on the conflicting forces of economic unity and ethnic division. It also stood for hierarchical power in the world – also outdated. At present, it sets a seal of 'genuine antique' on Britain. This feeds the tourist trade's love of fabricated folklore and the traffic in nostalgia. But it does very little to help us live here today – or tomorrow.

Simply to abolish the monarchy would not meet present needs, or cure deep and present ills; it might even exacerbate the fragmentation and disarray. But to reform it is vital, desirable, practical – and possible. A revised British monarchy could play a part in a new constitution, one limb in a body of law and rights which would strengthen British society, making its institutions meet people's potential as well as needs; the new monarchy might even be able to find a symbolic role in affirming that revolutionary but peaceful change, when subjects stop being subjects, and take their place and have their say as citizens.

DAVID MARQUAND

FOLLOWERS OR CITIZENS?

I THINK THAT there is a general recognition that the key issue in the debate about the monarchy, is really the British state. It's about the relationship between the British state and the British people. It's about the myths, the rituals, and the understandings which inform the rulers of the British state about who they are and how they ought to behave. Therefore it's a debate about us as a people – how we see ourselves and how we shape our own identity in the future.

I want to begin by making what seems to me to be an almost self-evident proposition, which is that the *existing* state, the *existing* network of understandings, rituals, and myths that we have known for so long, is now in a condition of crisis, or at least of severe disarray. If you look back over the history of this country for the last 30 years, what do you see? Well, you see first and foremost a quite extraordinary record of failure by the British state to achieve its own stated purposes in the economic sphere; a set of failures which goes far beyond party politics because it applies as much to the governments of the left as to the governments of the right. It applies as much to the governments of the 1980s and the 1990s as to the governments of the 1960s and 1970s. It doesn't seem to matter what economic theory the British state tries to operate by, it achieves failure just the same.

Secondly, it seems to me to be beyond dispute that the whole basis of the British state – the question of what it is, what territory it covers – is now in dispute in a sense which has not been true since it first came into existence in 1707. Remember that the British state only came into existence when Scotland voluntarily decided to join a union with England. Before that there was an *English* state, there was no *British* state. Now I think it is beyond dispute that the nature of the union is in serious contention for the first time since the eighteenth century. There isn't a revolutionary crisis. There aren't mobs parading in Edinburgh or Glasgow. Nobody is throwing bombs *there* – although there is a certain amount of unpleasantness in another part of the British state, namely in Northern Ireland –but there is a deep sense of alienation among the non-English nations of the United Kingdom (not just Scotland, but Wales too), and from the structures of the British state.

Thirdly, it is surely beyond dispute that the British state has found it extraordinarily difficult to make a success of its own desire to be part of a supranational European Community. One thing which has been common to all governments that have held power in this country since the early 1960s is that, rightly or wrongly, for better or worse, they have all believed that it was essential for Britain to be part of a supranational European Community. The other thing that has been common to all of them since we actually entered the Community in 1973, is that all of them have lied consistently to the British people about the implications of membership and none of them have made a success of it. Why is that? Obviously, there is no single cause; the problems facing all countries in Europe, not only ours, are extraordinarily difficult; constitutional change is not a panacea that is miraculously going to cure all ills. But I do suggest that one reason which is fundamental is a true erosion of trust between governments and governed, the steady ebbing of the legitimacy of the system, drip-by-drip, year-by-year. More and more the British people say to themselves, 'Why should we do what the government is asking us to do? What right have they got to carry through these laws? What right have they got to impose sacrifices upon us? We don't accept that they are acting in good faith. We don't believe them when they tell us the things that they tell us'.

I think that one reason for this – I only say it's one reason – is that the fundamental understandings which used to underpin the traditional constitution in this country have worn out. What was that understanding? It's really very simple. It was that politics, and the political community, were a matter of leaders and led. There were leaders and there were followers; the leaders led and the followers followed. That's what is still meant by the doctrine of absolute parliamentary sovereignty. Autonomous executive power is separate from civil society and public policy is not the property of the citizens. That system worked fine for a couple of hundred years in a deferential and rather homogeneous society. Most British people didn't get much benefit from it, but nevertheless it ruled an enormous and powerful empire stretching across the world. It doesn't work anymore, because people are no longer prepared to accept the legitimacy of arrangements which assume that leaders lead and followers follow.

A long time ago Tawney, perhaps the greatest exponent of the ideal of citizenship in this country in this century, said that Britain accepted democracy in the nineteenth and early twentieth centuries as a *convenience*, much like an improved system of telephones. She did not dedicate herself to it as the expression of a moral ideal and she went to the ballot box touching her hat. I think that is the problem in a nutshell. Now, at long last, the British people are saying that we are not prepared any longer to touch our hats; we actually demand citizenship. We demand to be governed according to the principles of a civic society. Of course, that demand can't be realised without a whole set of institutional changes. Institutions embody values, assumptions, myths, traditions; you can't get from here to there without institutional change. In fact, institutional change is only the outer shell, but it's indispensable if you want to create a proper civil society in this country. I think the time for change is long overdue and I congratulate Charter 88 for debating the future of the monarchy in the larger context, because I think it could prove a very big help to achieving this change.

CONTRIBUTORS

Martin Amis is a novelist and the author of *The Rachel Papers*, *Money*, *London Fields* and most recently *Visiting Mrs Nabokov*. He has written for the *New Statesman*, the *TLS* and the *Observer*.

Anthony Barnett is the Coordinator of Charter 88. Previously a writer and journalist, he is the author of *Iron Britannia* and *Soviet Freedom*, and conceived and helped to make the TV film *England's Henry Moore*.

Neil Belton is Deputy Publishing Director of Jonathan Cape.

Dr Vernon Bogdanor is Reader in Government at Oxford University and a Fellow of Brasenose College. He is currently writing a book on the monarchy and the constitution. Among his past publications are *Constitutions in Democratic Politics*, *What is Proportional Representation?*, and *The People and the Party Systems*.

Billy Bragg is an Essex-born rock singer. After a brief career as a goat herd and a stint in the Royal Armoured Corps, he first came to prominence in 1983 with his debut album, *Life's a Riot*. He has recorded several more albums including *Don't try this at Home*; *Talking with the Taxman about Poetry*; *Worker's Playtime*, *Brewing Up* and *Internationale*. He has performed in more than a thousand shows, in over 30 countries.

Jonathan Clark is a Fellow of All Souls College, Oxford and the author of a number of works of English history, including

Dynamics of Change, *Revolution and Rebellion*, *English Society 1688–1832*, and *The Language of Liberty*.

James Cornford is the Director of the Institute for Public Policy Research and oversaw the drafting of *The Constitution of the United Kingdom*, a model comprehensive draft with commentaries on what a British written constitution might be like.

Caroline Ellis is Charter 88's Political Officer. Along with Paul Hirst and Anthony Barnett she edited Charter 88's *Debating the Constitution*, published by Polity Press in 1993, and is currently co-editing a volume on the third wave of feminism.

James Fenton, author of *All the Wrong Places*, *The Snap Revolution* and *A Vacant Possession* amongst others, is a distinguished novelist, poet and journalist. His contribution is taken from a column in the *Independent*.

David Hare is one of Britain's best known and most prolific modern playwrights. His plays include *Absence of War* (on Labour and the 1992 General Election), *Murmuring Judges*, *Racing Demon*, *Heading Home*, and *The Secret Rapture* and he has directed plays at theatres throughout the country. He has also written for the cinema and television, such works as *Plenty*, *Wetherby* and *Paris by Night*.

Stephen Haseler is a professor of Politics and Modern History at London Guildhall University. He has written several books on politics including *The Politics of Giving*, *Battle for Britain: Thatcher and the New Liberals* and *The Tragedy of Labour*, and most recently *The Fall of the House of Windsor*. A founder member of the SDP, he is the Chair of Republic.

Christopher Hitchens is writer in residence with *Vanity Fair*, and has a regular column in *The Nation*, and is a frequent contributor to the *London Review of Books*. His most recent books are *Preparing for the Worst* and *Blood, Class and Nostalgia*.

Richard Hoggart is the author of many scholarly works including the pathbreaking *The Uses of Literacy*, *How and*

Why do we Learn, *Liberty and Legislation* and his autobiographical books, *A Sort of Clowning* and *An Imagined Life*.

Anthony Holden's *The Tarnished Crown* appeared in 1993. He has published and edited many translations including *Aeschylus' Agamemnon* and *The Greek Anthology* and is responsible for the translations of the operas Don Giovanni, La Boheme and The Barber of Seville. His other works include *A Princely Marriage*, *Of Presidents*, *Prime Ministers and Princes* and *Big Deal*.

Richard Holme (Lord Holme of Cheltenham CBE) is a distinguished Liberal Democrat life Peer and is currently Liberal Democrat spokesman on Northern Ireland. A co-founder of Charter 88 he is the author of *The People's Kingdom* and was formerly chairman of the Constitutional Reform Centre

Will Hutton is Economics Editor of the *Guardian* and an experienced television presenter. He is currently writing a book on the economic consequences of the British state.

Helena Kennedy QC is a criminal-law barrister, broadcaster and author. Her latest book, *Eve Was Framed*, was published in 1992, and is published by Vintage. Her work includes the award winning television drama *Blind Justice*. She is Chancellor of Oxford Brookes University, the Chair of Charter 88's Council and a member of its Executive.

Lady Longford, the well-known biographer of the Royal Family, was at one time 'an incipient republican', but her research into the life of Queen Victoria changed her into a 'fervent monarchist'. She has also written biographies of the Queen and the Queen Mother. Her most recent book is *Royal Throne: The Future of the Monarchy*.

David Marquand is Director of the Centre for Political Economy at Sheffield University, author of *The Unprincipled Society* and a member of the Charter 88 Council. A former Labour MP, he has worked for the European Commission in Brussels and currently serves on both Labour's Borrie

Commission on Social Justice and Ralph Dahrendorf's Liberal-Democrat Commission.

Charles Moore is Editor of the *Sunday Telegraph*. He is the author of *The Church in Crisis* and *A Tory Seer: The Selected Journalism of T E Utley*.

Andrew Morton is best known as the author of *Diana: Her True Story*, a book assaulted at the time as largely fabricated and recognised now as largely vindicated.

Tom Nairn is one of Scotland's and Britain's foremost political thinkers. He has a fortnightly column in *The Scotsman* and writes for television. His previous books include *The Break-up of Britain?*, *The Left Against Europe* and on the monarchy his pathbreaking *The Enchanted Glass*, published by Vintage. He has also written films for television, such as *Reid About Scotland* and *All About Everything*.

Tom Paulin is a poet and literary critic. He has edited several editions of poetry including the *Faber book of Political Verse* and the *Faber Book of Vernacular Verse* along with several editions of his own poetry, including *Five Mile Town*, *The Liberty Tree* and *Hillsborough Script*.

Claire Rayner is a writer and broadcaster who has worked on *Woman's Own*, the *Sun*, and the *Sunday Mirror*. She has also appeared on such television programmes as 'Pebble Mill at One', 'Claire Rayner's Casebook' and 'Advice Spot – TV-AM'. She has published prolifically on health and the family.

Geoffrey Robertson QC was the successful defence council in the Matrix Churchill trial that led to the Scott Inquiry. He is the author of the authoritative *Freedom, the Individual and the Law*.

Sir John Stokes was Conservative MP for Halesowen and Stourbridge from 1974 to 1992.

Carole Tongue is the Labour MEP for London East, and European Labour Party spokesperson on the car industry. She is also a member of the Co-operative Society, and on the Charter 88 Council.

Jack Straw MP is shadow Environment minister and Labour MP for Blackburn.

Sue Townsend is the author of, amongst other things, the best-selling *Adrian Mole* series and *The Queen and I* which has recently been turned into a play as well as having been serialised on Radio Four.

Hilary Wainwright is the political editor of *Red Pepper*, and Senior Research Fellow for International Labour Studies at Manchester University. Her most recent book is *Arguments for a New Left; Answering the Free Market Right*. She is a member of the Charter 88 Council.

Marina Warner is a novelist, whose books include *Mermaids in the Basement, Monuments and Maidens, Indigo* and *The Lost Father* which was shortlisted for the Booker Prize. She gave the 1994 Reith Lectures, *Managing Monsters, Six Myths of Our Time* which is published by Vintage and she is a member of Charter 88's Executive.

Fay Weldon's novels include *The Life and Loves of a She-Devil, Praxis, The Heart of the Country, Growing Rich*, and most recently *Affliction*. A former member of the Arts Council Literary Panel, as well as the Film and Video panel of the GLA, Fay Weldon was the Chair of the 1983 Booker Prize, and is now on the Video Censorship Appeals Committee.

Shirley Williams (**Baroness Williams of Crosby**) was co-founder and then President of the Social Democratic Party in 1981. She was a Labour Secretary of State for Education and Science, and is now Professor of Elective Politics at the John F Kennedy School of Government, Harvard University.

Patrick Wright, is an author and essayist, and frequent contributor to the *Guardian*. He is the author of *On Living in an Old Country* and *A Journey Through the Ruins*.

FOOTNOTES

[1] Peter Hennessey, *Searching For the Great Ghost*, his scintillating inaugural lecture, 1 February 1994. To be published in 1995.

[2] I am indebted to Richard Shepherd MP for information on this.

[3] Godfrey Hodgson, *The Electoral Register: A Squinting Eye to Democracy*, no.8 in Charter 88 series *Violations of Rights in Britain*.

[4] Thomas Paine, *The Rights of Man*, p.136, Penguin edition, Harmondsworth 1969.

[5] Lord Scarman, *Why Britain Needs a Written Constitution*, fourth Charter 88 Sovereignty Lecture, July 1992. All Sovereignty Lectures are available from Charter 88 at £2.50 each.

[6] *Sunday Telegraph*, 12 December 1993.

[7] David Cannadine, 'The British Monarchy and the Invention of Tradition' in Eric Hobsbawm and Terence Ranger, *The Invention of Tradition*, Cambridge 1983.

[8] Linda Colley, *Britons: The Forging of a Nation*, 1993, p.233.

[9] Anthony Holden, *The Tarnished Crown*, London 1993, p.48.

[10] A full version of Michael Portillo's speech was published in the *Independent on Sunday*, 16 January 1994.

[11] *The Times*, 30 July 1993.

[12] Andrew Morton, *Diana: Her True Story*, chapter 8 especially, London 1992.

[13] Matthew Parris, *The Times*, 13 February 1993.

[14] Walter Bagehot, *The English Constitution*, London 1963 introduced by Richard Crossman, pp. 105, 86, 69, 65

[15] As above pp.219, 87 and 97.

[16] Robert Rhodes James's 'The British Monarchy; its changing constitutional role', lecture and discussion, *RSA Journal* April 1994.

[17] Ferdinand Mount, *The British Constitution Now Recovery or Decline?*, 1992, pp.35, 31 and 28.

[18] Introduction to Walter Bagehot, *The English Constitution*, as above p.33.

[19] P.J Cain and A.G Hopkins, *British Imperialism Vol.I: Innovation and Expansion 1688–1914*, and Vol. II *Crisis and Deconstruction 1914–1990*, London 1993, Vol. II p.299.

[20] 'The triumphs of the past have become the bane of the present' - see Perry Anderson's brilliant essay of 1964, *Origins of the Present Crisis*, which predates the long research of Cain and Hopkins and deserves to be acknowledged for its pioneering perceptions. It can be found in his *English Questions*, London 1992.

[21] Cain and Hopkins, as above, Vol. II, p.300.

[22] Jim Bulpitt, *Territory and Power in British Politics*, Manchester, 1983.

[23] Eric Evans, *The Great Reform Act of 1832*, London 1983.

[24] Thomas Hobbes, *Leviathan*, ed. Macpherson, 1968 edition, p.228. See also David Held, *Models of Democracy*, Polity Press, Cambridge 1987.

[25] Lord Hailsham, *On the Constitution*, London 1992, p.105.

[26] As above p.94.

[27] I have written a fuller description of 'Churchillism' in Chapter three of *Iron Britannia: Why Parliament Fought its Falklands War*, London 1982.

[28] Paul Hirst, *Associative Democracy*, Polity Press, Cambridge 1993.

[29] Margaret Thatcher, *The Downing Street Years*, London 1993, p.6.

[30] See David Marquand, *The Unprincipled Society*, London 1988, pp.68 and 176.

[31] Malcolm Rifkind, quoted by Peter Henessy (see note 1) and Geoffrey Howe, review of *The Downing Street Years*, in *Financial Times*, 23 October 1993.

[32] Neal Ascherson, *Local Government and the Myth of Sovereignty*, Charter 88 Sovereignty Lecture, May 1994, (see footnote 5)

[33] See Tom Nairn's new introduction to *The Enchanted Glass*, in the Vintage paperback edition, 1994.

[34] Charles Handy, *The Empty Raincoat*, London 1994. See especially the section on federalist forms of organisation pp.97-128.

[35] Gordon Brown, *Constitutional Change and the Future of Britain*, first Charter 88 Sovereignty Lecture, March 1992 (see footnote 5).

[36] Martin Jacques, *The End of Politics*, *Sunday Times*, 18 July 1993.

[37] William Shawcross, *Rupert Murdoch: Ringmaster of the Information Circus*. London, 1992 p.552.

[38] Anthony Barnett, Caroline Ellis and Paul Hirst, *Debating the Constitution: New Perspectives on Constitutional Reform*, London, Polity Press, Cambridge 1993.

[39] *The Democratic Audit of the United Kingdom*, edited by Kevin Boyle and Stuart Weir, Routledge, forthcoming 1995.

ACKNOWLEDGEMENTS

MANY THANKS TO all those who worked on the book as a whole:

Sarah Aitkin, Neil Belton, Harry Cocks, Kevin Davey, Janet Hall, Judith Herrin, Isobel Hitchcock, Susanna Johnstone, Juliet Rawlins, Tania Rose.

And to those who gave special help on Anthony Barnett's Introduction:

Neil Belton, Harry Cocks, Janet Hall, Judith Herrin, Paul Hirst, John Pipal, Marina Warner, Stuart Weir.

The book would not have happened without the conference, on *The Monarchy, the Constitution and the People* held in London on 22 May 1993. Thanks are due to Jane Powell, Lindsay Cooke, Sarah Aitkin, their team of helpers and volunteers, to all the speakers and to the consultants including Tim Miller (Chair), Matt D'Ancona, Caroline Michel, Mary-Ann Seighart, Sue Townsend, Edgar Wilson and the 500 participants.

Special thanks to *The Times*, who sponsored the conference, and in particular Peter Stothard. And thanks to *Vanity Fair*, Random House, and the Paul Hamlyn Foundation.

We would like to thank Channel 4 for the programme of the conference, The Queen and Us.

Without the support of the Charter 88 staff, volunteers and Executive throughout the creation of the book, it could not have been completed.

CHARTER 88

If you would like to know more about Charter 88 you can write to: Charter 88, FREEPOST (ED0 5005), London EC1B 1ZT.

CHARTER 88's demands are:-
A Bill of Rights
Freedom of Information
Accountable Government
A reformed House of Commons
A democratic Upper House
Reform of the Judiciary
Redress for all State Abuse
Independence for local government
Scottish and Welsh Parliaments
Devolution of Power
A Written Constitution

The inscription of laws does not guarantee their realisation. Only people themselves can ensure freedom, democracy and equality before the law. Nonetheless, such ends are far better demanded, and more effectively obtained and guarded, once they belong to everyone by inalienable right.